www.EffortlessMath.com

... So Much More Online!

✓ FREE Math lessons

✓ More Math learning books!

✓ Mathematics Worksheets

✓ Online Math Tutors

Need a PDF version of this book?

Please visit www.EffortlessMath.com

5 Full-Length Praxis Core Math Practice Tests

The Practice You Need to Ace the Praxis Core Math (5733) Test

By

Reza Nazari & Ava Ross

Copyright © 2020

Reza Nazari & Ava Ross

All inquiries should be addressed to:

info@effortlessMath.com

www.EffortlessMath.com

ISBN: 978-1-64612-427-5

Published by: Effortless Math Education

www.EffortlessMath.com

Description

5 Full-Length Praxis Core Math Practice Tests, which reflects the 2020 and 2021 test guidelines and topics, is designed to help you hone your math skills, overcome your exam anxiety, and boost your confidence -- and do your best to ace the Praxis Core Math (5733) Test. The realistic and full-length Praxis Core Math tests show you how the test is structured and what math topics you need to master. The practice test questions are followed by answer explanations to help you find your weak areas, learn from your mistakes, and raise your Praxis Core Math (5733) score.

The surest way to succeed on Praxis Core Math Test is with intensive practice in every math topic tested-- and that's what you will get in *5 Full-Length Praxis Core Math Practice Tests*. This Praxis Math new edition has been updated to replicate questions appearing on the most recent Praxis Core Math tests. This is a precious learning tool for Praxis Math test takers who need extra practice in math to improve their Praxis Core Math (5733) score. After taking the Praxis Core Math practice tests in this book, you will have solid foundation and adequate practice that is necessary to succeed on the Praxis Core Math test. **This book is your ticket to ace the Praxis Core Math Test!**

5 Full-Length Praxis Core Math Practice Tests contains many exciting and unique features to help you improve your test scores, including:

- Content 100% aligned with the 2020 - 2021 Praxis Core Math (5733) test

- Written by Praxis Core Math tutors and test experts

- Complete coverage of all Praxis Core Math concepts and topics which you will be tested

- Detailed answers and explanations for every Praxis Core Math practice questions to help you learn from your mistakes

- 5 full-length practice tests (featuring new question types) with detailed answers

This Praxis Core Math book and other Effortless Math Education books are used by thousands of test-takers each year to help them review core content areas, brush-up in math, discover their strengths and weaknesses, and achieve their best scores on the Praxis Core test.

About the Author

Reza Nazari is the author of more than 100 Math learning books including:
– **Math and Critical Thinking Challenges:** For the Middle and High School Student
– **GRE Math in 30 Days**
– **ASVAB Math Workbook 2018 - 2019**
– **Effortless Math Education Workbooks**
– **and many more Mathematics books …**

Reza is also an experienced Math instructor and a test–prep expert who has been tutoring students since 2008. Reza is the founder of Effortless Math Education, a tutoring company that has helped many students raise their standardized test scores—and attend the colleges of their dreams. Reza provides an individualized custom learning plan and the personalized attention that makes a difference in how students view math.

You can contact Reza via email at:
reza@EffortlessMath.com

Find Reza's professional profile at:
goo.gl/zoC9rJ

Contents

Praxis Core Test Review

The Praxis Core Academic Skills for Educators is a standardized test used for admissions to teacher preparation programs in the United States. In essence, it is a broad and quick assessment of students' academic abilities. The exam was designed and is administered by the Educational Testing Service (ETS) and scoring well on this exam is vital to being accepted for admission into teacher preparation programs.

The Praxis Core test covers three topics.

- Math
- Reading
- Writing

The Praxis Core Math (5733) is comprised of 56 multiple choice and numeric entry questions and test takers have 90 minutes to answer the questions. You will be able to use a basic on-screen calculator on Praxis Core Math test.

Praxis Core Mathematics cover the following topics:

- Number and Quantity (36%)
- Algebra and Functions (20%)
- Geometry (12%)
- Data Interpretation, Statistics and Probability (32%)

In this book, there are five complete Praxis Core Math Tests. Take these tests to see what score you'll be able to receive on a real Praxis Core Math test.

Good luck!

Time to Test

Time to refine your quantitative reasoning skill with a practice test

Take a Praxis Core Math test to simulate the test day experience. After you've finished, score your test using the answer keys.

Before You Start

- You'll need a pencil, a calculator and a timer to take the test.

- For each question, there are five possible answers. Choose which one is best.

- It's okay to guess. There is no penalty for wrong answers.

- After you've finished the test, review the answer key to see where you went wrong.

Good Luck!

Praxis Core Math (5733)
Practice Test 1

2020- 2021

Total number of questions: 56

Total time: 90 Minutes

You may use a calculator on this practice test.

(On a real Praxis test, there is an onscreen calculator to use.)

1) In five successive hours, a car traveled $40\ km, 45\ km, 50\ km, 35\ km$ and $55\ km$. In the next five hours, it traveled with an average speed of $65\ km\ per\ hour$. Find the total distance the car traveled in 10 hours.
   A. $425\ km$
   B. $450\ km$
   C. $550\ km$
   D. $600\ km$
   E. $1,000\ km$

2) How long does a 420–miles trip take moving at 65 miles per hour (mph)?
   A. $4\ hours$
   B. $6\ hours\ and\ 24\ minutes$
   C. $8\ hours\ and\ 24\ minutes$
   D. $8\ hours\ and\ 30\ minutes$
   E. $10\ hours\ and\ 30\ minutes$

3) Right triangle ABC has two legs of lengths $5\ cm\ (AB)$ and $12\ cm$ (AC). What is the length of the third side (BC)?
   A. $4\ cm$
   B. $6\ cm$
   C. $8\ cm$
   D. $13\ cm$
   E. $20\ cm$

Gender	Under 45	45 or older	total
Male	12	6	18
Female	5	7	12
Total	17	13	30

4) The table above shows the distribution of age and gender for 30 employees in a company. If one employee is selected at random, what is the probability that the employee selected be either a female under age 45 or a male age 45 or older?
   A. $\dfrac{5}{6}$
   B. $\dfrac{5}{30}$
   C. $\dfrac{6}{30}$
   D. $\dfrac{11}{30}$
   E. $\dfrac{17}{30}$

5) $(7x + 2y)(5x + 2y) = ?$
 A. $2x^2 + 14xy + 2y^2$
 B. $2x^2 + 4xy + 2y^2$
 C. $7x^2 + 14xy + y^2$
 D. $10x^2 + 14xy + 4y$
 E. $35x^2 + 24xy + 4y^2$

6) Which of the following expressions is equivalent to $5x\,(4 + 2y)$?
 A. $x + 10xy$
 B. $5x + 5xy$
 C. $20xy + 2xy$
 D. $20x + 5xy$
 E. $20x + 10xy$

7) If $y = 5ab + 3b^3$, what is y when $a = 2$ and $b = 3$?
 A. 24
 B. 31
 C. 36
 D. 51
 E. 111

8) From the figure, which of the following must be true? (figure not drawn to scale)

 A. $y = z$
 B. $y = 5x$
 C. $y \geq x$
 D. $y + 4x = z$
 E. $y > x$

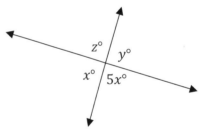

9) The perimeter of the trapezoid below is 64. What is its area?
 A. $252\ cm^2$
 B. $234\ cm^2$
 C. $216\ cm^2$
 D. $154\ cm^2$
 E. $260\ cm^2$

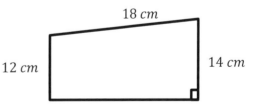

18 cm

12 cm

14 cm

10) Two third of 15 is equal to $\frac{2}{5}$ of what number?
 A. 12
 B. 20
 C. 25
 D. 60
 E. 90

11) The marked price of a computer is D dollar. Its price decreased by 25% in January and later increased by 10% in February. What is the final price of the computer in D dollar?
   A. 0.80 D
   B. 0.82 D
   C. 0.90 D
   D. 1.20 D
   E. 1.40 D

12) In the following equation, what is the value of $y - 3x$?

$$\frac{y}{5} = x - \frac{2}{5}x + 2$$

   Write your answer in the box below.

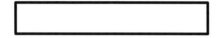

13) What is the value of x in the following equation?

$$\frac{x^2-16}{x+4} + 3(x + 4) = 15$$

   Write your answer in the box below.

14) The length of a rectangle is 3 meters greater than 4 times its width. The perimeter of the rectangle is 36 meters. What is the area of the rectangle in meters?

   Write your answer in the box below.

15) The area of a circle is 49 π. What is the circumference of the circle?
   A. 7 π
   B. 14 π
   C. 32 π
   D. 64 π
   E. 124 π

16) A $50 shirt now selling for $28 is discounted by what percent?
    A. 20%
    B. 44%
    C. 54%
    D. 60%
    E. 80%

17) In 1999, the average worker's income increased $2,000 per year starting from $26,000 annual salary. Which equation represents income greater than average? (I = income, x = number of years after 1999)
    A. $I > 2000\,x + 26000$
    B. $I > -2000\,x + 26000$
    C. $I < -2000\,x + 26000$
    D. $I < 2000\,x - 26000$
    E. $I < 24{,}000\,x + 26000$

18) A boat sails 60 miles south and then 80 miles east. How far is the boat from its start point?
    A. $45\ miles$
    B. $50\ miles$
    C. $60\ miles$
    D. $70\ miles$
    E. $100\ miles$

19) Sophia purchased a sofa for $530.40. The sofa is regularly priced at $631. What was the percent discount Sophia received on the sofa?
    A. 12%
    B. 16%
    C. 20%
    D. 25%
    E. 40%

20) The score of Emma was half as that of Ava and the score of Mia was twice that of Ava. If the score of Mia was 40, what is the score of Emma?
    A. 10
    B. 15
    C. 20
    D. 30
    E. 40

21) A bag contains 18 balls: two green, five black, eight blue, a brown, a red and one white. If 17 balls are removed from the bag at random, what is the probability that a brown ball has been removed?

   A. $\frac{1}{9}$

   B. $\frac{1}{6}$

   C. $\frac{16}{18}$

   D. $\frac{17}{18}$

   E. $\frac{1}{2}$

22) The average of five consecutive numbers is 36. What is the smallest number?
   A. 38
   B. 36
   C. 34
   D. 12
   E. 8

23) The price of a car was $28,000 in 2012. In 2013, the price of that car was $18,200. What was the rate of depreciation of the price of car per year?
   A. 20%
   B. 30%
   C. 35%
   D. 40%
   E. 50%

24) The width of a box is one third of its length. The height of the box is one third of its width. If the length of the box is 36 cm, what is the volume of the box?
   A. $81\ cm^3$
   B. $162\ cm^3$
   C. $243\ cm^3$
   D. $1,728\ cm^3$
   E. $1,880\ cm^3$

25) A tree 32 feet tall casts a shadow 12 feet long. Jack is 6 feet tall. How long is Jack's shadow?
   A. $2.25\ feet$
   B. $4\ feet$
   C. $4.25\ feet$
   D. $8\ feet$
   E. $12\ feet$

26) When a number is subtracted from 28 and the difference is divided by that number, the result is 3. What is the value of the number?
   A. 2
   B. 4
   C. 7
   D. 12
   E. 24

27) An angle is equal to one ninth of its supplement. What is the measure of that angle?
   A. 9
   B. 18
   C. 25
   D. 60
   E. 90

28) John traveled 150 km in 6 hours and Alice traveled 140 km in 4 hours. What is the ratio of the average speed of John to average speed of Alice?
   A. 3 : 2
   B. 2 : 3
   C. 5 : 7
   D. 5 : 6
   E. 11 : 16

29) What is the value of this expression? $[3 \times (-14) - 48] - (-14) + [3 \times 8] \div 2$

   Write your answer in the box below.

   ⬚

30) If $x - 4(x + 2) = -15.5$, what is the value of x?

   Write your answer in the box below.

   ⬚

31) The following graph shows the mark of six students in mathematics. What is the mean (average) of the marks?

A. 15
B. 14.14
C. 14
D. 13.5
E. 11.5

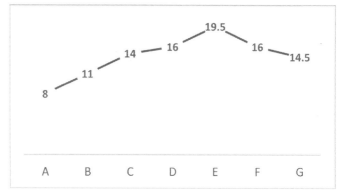

32) A chemical solution contains 6% alcohol. If there is 24 ml of alcohol, what is the volume of the solution?
A. 240 ml
B. 400 ml
C. 600 ml
D. 1,200 ml
E. 2,400 ml

33) The average weight of 18 girls in a class is 56 kg and the average weight of 32 boys in the same class is 62 kg. What is the average weight of all the 50 students in that class?
A. 50
B. 59.84
C. 61.68
D. 61.90
E. 62.20

34) The price of a laptop is decreased by 20% to $360. What is its original price?
A. $320
B. $380
C. $400
D. $450
E. $500

35) A bank is offering 4.5% simple interest on a savings account. If you deposit $9,000, how much interest will you earn in five years?
A. $360
B. $720
C. $2,025
D. $3,600
E. $4,800

36) Multiply and write the product in scientific notation:
$$(2.9 \times 10^6) \times (2.6 \times 10^{-5})$$
   A. 754×100
   B. 75.4×10^6
   C. 75.4×10^{-5}
   D. 7.54×10^{11}
   E. 7.54×10

37) If the height of a right pyramid is $14\ cm$ and its base is a square with side $6\ cm$. What is its volume?
   A. $432\ cm^3$
   B. $3088\ cm^3$
   C. $236\ cm^3$
   D. $172\ cm^3$
   E. $168\ cm^3$

38) 5 less than twice a positive integer is 73. What is the integer?
   A. 39
   B. 41
   C. 42
   D. 44
   E. 50

39) A shirt costing $300 is discounted 15%. After a month, the shirt is discounted another 15%. Which of the following expressions can be used to find the selling price of the shirt?
   A. $(300)\,(0.70)$
   B. $(300) - 300\,(0.30)$
   C. $(300)(0.15) - (300)\,(0.15)$
   D. $(300)\,(0.85)(0.85)$
   E. $(300)(0.85)(0.85) - (300)\,(0.15)$

40) Which of the following points lies on the line $2x + 4y = 8$?
   A. $(2, 1)$
   B. $(-1, 3)$
   C. $(-2, 2)$
   D. $(2, 2)$
   E. $(2, 8)$

41) If $2x + 2y = 2$, $3x - y = 7$, which of the following ordered pairs (x, y) satisfies both equations?
   A. $(1, 3)$
   B. $(2, 4)$
   C. $(2, -1)$
   D. $(4, -6)$
   E. $(1, -6)$

42) If $f(x) = 3x + 4(x + 1) + 2$ then $f(4x) = ?$
   A. $28x + 6$
   B. $16x - 6$
   C. $25x + 4$
   D. $12x + 3$
   E. $12x - 3$

43) A line in the xy-plane passes through origin and has a slope of $\frac{1}{3}$. Which of the following points lies on the line?
   A. $(2,1)$
   B. $(4,1)$
   C. $(9,3)$
   D. $(6,3)$
   E. $(1,3)$

44) Which of the following is equivalent to $(3n^2 + 2n + 6) - (2n^2 - 4)$?
   A. $n + 4n^2$
   B. $n^2 - 3$
   C. $n^2 + 2n + 10$
   D. $n + 2$
   E. $n - 2$

45) Solve for x: $4(x + 1) = 6(x - 4) + 20$
   A. 12
   B. 6.5
   C. 4
   D. 2
   E. 0

46) If $x \neq -4$ and $x \neq 5$, which of the following is equivalent to $\dfrac{1}{\frac{1}{x-5}+\frac{1}{x+4}}$?

A. $\dfrac{(x-5)(x+4)}{(x-5)+(x+4)}$

B. $\dfrac{(x+4)+(x-5)}{(x+4)(x-5)}$

C. $\dfrac{(x+4)(x-5)}{(x+4)-(x+5)}$

D. $\dfrac{(x+4)+(x-5)}{(x+4)-(x-5)}$

E. $\dfrac{(x-4)+(x-5)}{(x+4)-(x-5)}$

$$y < c - x \,,\, y > x + b$$

47) In the xy-plane, if $(0,0)$ is a solution to the system of inequalities above, which of the following relationships between c and b must be true?

A. $c < b$
B. $c > b$
C. $c = b$
D. $c = b + c$
E. $c = b - x$

48) What is the value of x in the following equation? $3x + 10 = 46$

A. 4
B. 7
C. 10
D. 12
E. 16

49) Calculate $f(5)$ for the following function f.

$$f(x) = x^2 - 3x$$

A. 5

B. 10

C. 15

D. 20

E. 25

50) If $\frac{4}{x} = \frac{12}{x-8}$ what is the value of $\frac{x}{2}$?

    A. 1

    B. 3

    C. -2

    D. 2

    E. 0

51) What is the perimeter of a square in centimeters that has an area of $595.36\ cm^2$?

    Write your answer in the box below. (don't write the measurement)

52) A swimming pool holds 2,000 cubic feet of water. The swimming pool is 25 feet long and 10 feet wide. How deep is the swimming pool?

    Write your answer in the box below. (<u>Don't write the measurement</u>)

53) The circle graph below shows all Mr. Green's expenses for last month. If he spent $660 on his car, how much did he spend for his rent?

    A. $700

    B. $740

    C. $810

    D. $910

    E. $960

Mr. Green's monthly expenses

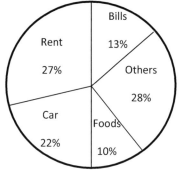

54) A function $g(3) = 5$ and $g(5) = 4$. A function $f(5) = 2$ and $f(4) = 6$. What is the value of $f(g(5))$?

    A. 5

    B. 6

    C. 7

    D. 8

    E. 10

55) What is the area of the following equilateral triangle if the side $AB = 12\ cm$?

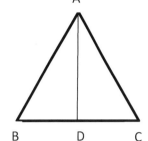

    A. $36\sqrt{3}\ cm^2$
    B. $18\sqrt{3}\ cm^2$
    C. $6\sqrt{3}\ cm^2$
    D. $8\ cm^2$
    E. $6\ cm^2$

56) If $x \blacksquare y = \sqrt{x^2 + y}$, what is the value of $6 \blacksquare 28$?

    A. $\sqrt{168}$
    B. 10
    C. 8
    D. 6
    E. 4

End of Praxis Core Math Practice Test 1

Praxis Core Math (5733) Practice Test 2

2020- 2021

Total number of questions: 56

Total time: 90 Minutes

You may use a calculator on this practice test.

(On a real Praxis test, there is an onscreen calculator to use.)

1) The mean of 50 test scores was calculated as 90. But, it turned out that one of the scores was misread as 94 but it was 69. What is the mean?
   A. 85
   B. 87
   C. 89.5
   D. 90.5
   E. 95.5

2) Two dice are thrown simultaneously, what is the probability of getting a sum of 5 or 8?
   A. $\frac{1}{3}$
   B. $\frac{11}{36}$
   C. $\frac{1}{16}$
   D. $\frac{1}{4}$
   E. $\frac{1}{36}$

3) Which of the following is equal to the expression below?

$$(5x + 2y)(2x - y)$$

   A. $4x^2 - 2y^2$
   B. $2x^2 + 6xy - 2y^2$
   C. $24x^2 + 2xy - 2y^2$
   D. $10x^2 - xy - 2y^2$
   E. $8x^2 + 2xy - 2y^2$

4) What is the product of all possible values of x in the following equation?

$$|x - 10| = 4$$

   A. 3
   B. 7
   C. 13
   D. 84
   E. 100

5) What is the slope of a line that is perpendicular to the line $4x - 2y = 6$?
   A. -2
   B. $-\frac{1}{2}$
   C. 4
   D. 12
   E. 14

6) What is the value of the expression $6(x - 2y) + (2 - x)^2$ when $x = 3$ and $y = -2$?
   A. -4
   B. 20
   C. 43
   D. 50
   E. 80

7) A swimming pool holds 2,500 cubic feet of water. The swimming pool is 25 feet long and 10 feet wide. How deep is the swimming pool?
   A. $2\ feet$
   B. $4\ feet$
   C. $6\ feet$
   D. $7\ feet$
   E. $10\ feet$

8) Four one – foot rulers can be split among how many users to leave each with $\frac{1}{3}$ of a ruler?
   A. 4
   B. 6
   C. 12
   D. 24
   E. 48

9) What is the area of a square whose diagonal is 4?
   A. 4
   B. 8
   C. 16
   D. 64
   E. 124

10) The average of five numbers is 26. If a sixth number 42 is added, then, what is the new average? (round your answer to the nearest hundredth)
   A. 25
   B. 26.5
   C. 27
   D. 28.66
   E. 36

Questions 11 to 13 are based on the following data

The result of a research shows the number of men and women in four cities of a country.

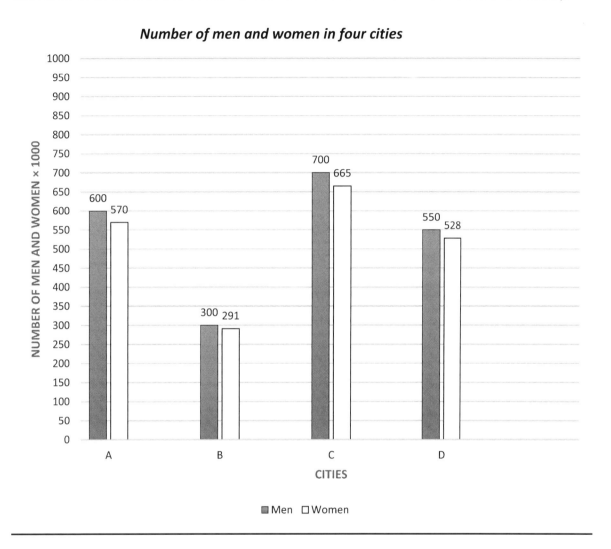

Number of men and women in four cities

11) What's the maximum ratio of the number of women to number of men in each city?

A. 0.98

B. 0.97

C. 0.96

D. 0.95

E. 0.94

12) What's the ratio of the percentage of men in city A to percentage of women in city C?

    A. $\frac{10}{9}$

    B. $\frac{9}{10}$

    C. 1

    D. $\frac{19}{20}$

    E. $\frac{20}{19}$

13) How many women should be added to city D to change the ratio of women to men to 1.2?

    A. 130

    B. 129

    C. 132

    D. 131

    E. 133

14) Jason needs an 70% average in his writing class to pass. On his first 4 exams, he earned scores of 68%, 72%, 85%, and 90%. What is the minimum score Jason can earn on his fifth and final test to pass?

    A. 80%,

    B. 70%

    C. 68%

    D. 54%

    E. 35%

15) What is the value of x in the following equation? $\frac{2}{3}x + \frac{1}{6} = \frac{1}{2}$

    A. 6

    B. $\frac{1}{2}$

    C. $\frac{1}{3}$

    D. $\frac{1}{4}$

    E. $\frac{1}{12}$

16) A bank is offering 4.5% simple interest on a savings account. If you deposit $12,000, how much interest will you earn in two years?

    A. $420

    B. $1,080

    C. $4,200

    D. $8,400

    E. $9,600

17) Simplify $7x^2y^3(2x^2y)^3 =$

    A. $12x^4y^6$
    B. $12x^8y^6$
    C. $56x^4y^6$
    D. $56x^8y^6$
    E. $96x^8y^6$

18) In the diagram below, circle A represents the set of all even numbers, circle B represents the set of all negative numbers, and circle C represents the set of all multiples of 6. Which number could be replaced with y?

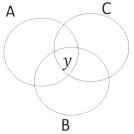

    A. 6
    B. 0
    C. -6
    D. -10
    E. -13

19) Last week 25,000 fans attended a football match. This week three times as many bought tickets, but one sixth of them cancelled their tickets. How many are attending this week?
    A. 48,000
    B. 54,000
    C. 62,500
    D. 75,000
    E. 84,000

20) What is the perimeter of a square that has an area of 49 square inches?
    A. $144\ inches$
    B. $64\ inches$
    C. $56\ inches$
    D. $48\ inches$
    E. $28\ inches$

21) If $f(x)=2x^3+5x^2+2x$ and $g(x)=-4$, what is the value of $f(g(x))$?

    A. 56
    B. 32
    C. 24
    D. -4
    E. -56

22) A cruise line ship left Port A and traveled 50 miles due west and then 120 miles due north. At this point, what is the shortest distance from the cruise to port A?
   A. 70 $miles$
   B. 80 $miles$
   C. 150 $miles$
   D. 230 $miles$
   E. 130 $miles$

23) What is the equivalent temperature of $104°F$ in Celsius?

$$C = \frac{5}{9}(F - 32)$$

   A. 32
   B. 40
   C. 48
   D. 52
   E. 64

24) The perimeter of a rectangular yard is 72 meters. What is its length if its width is twice its length?
   A. 12 $meters$
   B. 18 $meters$
   C. 20 $meters$
   D. 24 $meters$
   E. 36 $meters$

25) The average of 6 numbers is 14. The average of 4 of those numbers is 10. What is the average of the other two numbers?
   A. 10
   B. 12
   C. 14
   D. 22
   E. 24

26) If 150% of a number is 75, then what is the 80% of that number?
   A. 40
   B. 50
   C. 70
   D. 85
   E. 90

27) What is the slope of the line: $4x - 2y = 12$
   A. -1
   B. -2
   C. 1
   D. 1.5
   E. 2

28) In two successive years, the population of a town is increased by 10% and 20%. What percent of the population is increased after two years?
   A. 30%
   B. 32%
   C. 35%
   D. 68%
   E. 70%

29) The area of a circle is 36π. What is the diameter of the circle?
   A. 4
   B. 8
   C. 12
   D. 14
   E. 16

30) If 20% of a number is 4, what is the number?
   A. 4
   B. 8
   C. 10
   D. 20
   E. 25

31) If a tree casts a 26–foot shadow at the same time that a 3 feet yardstick casts a 2–foot shadow, what is the height of the tree?

   A. $24\,ft$
   B. $28\,ft$
   C. $39\,ft$
   D. $48\,ft$
   E. $52\,ft$

32) Jason is 9 miles ahead of Joe running at 6.5 miles per hour and Joe is running at the speed of 8 miles per hour. How long does it take Joe to catch Jason?
   A. $3\,hours$
   B. $4\,hours$
   C. $6\,hours$
   D. $8\,hours$
   E. $10\,hours$

33) 44 students took an exam and 11 of them failed. What percent of the students passed the exam?

$\frac{33}{44} = 75$

   A. 20%
   B. 40%
   C. 60%
   D. 75%
   E. 90%

34) If $f(x) = 2x^3 + 5x^2 + 2x$ and $g(x) = -3$, what is the value of $f(g(x))$?

   A. 36
   B. 32
   C. 24
   D. 15
   E. -15

35) The diagonal of a rectangle is 10 inches long and the height of the rectangle is 6 inches. What is the perimeter of the rectangle?

   A. $10\ inches$
   B. $12\ inches$
   C. $16\ inches$
   D. $18\ inches$
   E. $28\ inches$

36) The perimeter of the trapezoid below is $40\ cm$. What is its area?

   A. $48\ cm^2$
   B. $98\ cm^2$
   C. $140\ cm^2$
   D. $576\ cm^2$
   E. $986\ cm^2$

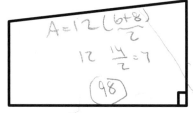

37) If $f(x) = 2x^3 + 2$ and $(x) = \frac{1}{x}$, what is the value of $f(g(x))$?

   A. $\dfrac{1}{2x^3+2}$

   B. $\dfrac{2}{x^3}$

   C. $\dfrac{1}{2x}$

   D. $\dfrac{1}{2x+2}$

   E. $\dfrac{2}{x^3}+2$

38) A cruise line ship left Port A and traveled 80 miles due west and then 150 miles due north.

At this point, what is the shortest distance from the cruise to port A?

    A. 70 miles

    B. 80 miles

    C. 150 miles

    D. 170 miles

    E. 230 miles

39) If the ratio of $5a$ to $2b$ is $\frac{1}{10}$, what is the ratio of a to b?

    A. 10

    B. 25

    C. $\frac{1}{25}$

    D. $\frac{1}{20}$

    E. $\frac{1}{10}$

40) If $x = 9$, what is the value of y in the following equation? $2y = \frac{2x^2}{3} + 6$

    A. 30

    B. 45

    C. 60

    D. 120

    E. 180

$$2y = \frac{2(81)+6}{3}$$

$$2y = \frac{162}{3} + 6$$

$$2y = 54 + 6$$

$$2y = 60 \quad y = 30$$

41) If $\frac{x-3}{5} = N$ and $N = 6$, what is the value of x?

    A. 25

    B. 28

    C. 30

    D. 33

    E. 36

42) Which of the following is equal to $b^{\frac{3}{5}}$?

   A. $\sqrt{b^{\frac{5}{3}}}$

   B. $b^{\frac{5}{3}}$

   C. $\sqrt[5]{b^3}$

   D. $\sqrt[3]{b^5}$

   E. $\sqrt[3]{b^{-5}}$

43) On Saturday, Sara read N pages of a book each hour for 3 hours, and Mary read M pages of a book each hour for 4 hours. Which of the following represents the total number of pages of book read by Sara and Mary on Saturday?

   A. $12MN$

   B. $3N + 4M$

   C. $7MN$

   D. $4N + 3M$

   E. $4N - 3M$

44) The average of five numbers is 25. If a sixth number that is greater than 42 is added, then, which of the following could be the new average? (Select one or more answer choices)

   A. 25

   B. 26

   C. 27

   D. 28

   E. 42

45) The diagonal of a rectangle is 10 inches long and the height of the rectangle is 8 inches. What is the perimeter of the rectangle in inches?
Write your answer in the box below.

46) Find the solution (x, y) to the following system of equations?
$$2x + 5y = 11$$
$$4x - 2y = -14$$
    A. $(14, 5)$
    B. $(6, 8)$
    C. $(11, 17)$
    D. $(-2, 3)$
    E. $(2, 3)$

47) Calculate $f(4)$ for the function $f(x) = 3x^2 - 4$.
    A. 44
    B. 40
    C. 38
    D. 30
    E. 20

48) What are the zeroes of the function $f(x) = x^3 + 5x^2 + 6x$?

    A. 0
    B. 2
    C. $0, 2, 3$
    D. $0, -2, -3$
    E. $0, -2, 3$

49) What is the value of the expression? $5 + 8 \times (-2) - [4 + 22 \times 5] \div 6$
Write your answer in the box below.

50) In the xy-plane, the point $(1, 2)$ and $(-1, 6)$ are on line A. Which of the following points could also be on line A? (Select one or more answer choices)
    A. $(-1, 2)$

    B. $(5, 7)$

    C. $(3, 4)$

    D. $(3, -2)$

    E. $(6, -8)$

51) The function $g(x)$ is defined by a polynomial. Some values of x and $g(x)$ are shown in the table below. Which of the following must be a factor of $g(x)$?

x	$g(x)$
0	5
1	4
2	0

A. x
B. $x - 1$
C. $x - 2$
D. $x + 1$
E. $x + 6$

52) What is the value of $\frac{4b}{c}$ when $\frac{c}{b} = 2$

A. 8
B. 4
C. 2
D. 1
E. 0

53) If $x + 5 = 8$, $2y - 1 = 5$ then $xy + 10 =$

A. 30
B. 24
C. 21
D. 17
E. 15

54) If $\frac{a-b}{b} = \frac{10}{13}$, then which of the following must be true?

A. $\frac{a}{b} = \frac{10}{13}$
B. $\frac{a}{b} = \frac{23}{13}$
C. $\frac{a}{b} = \frac{13}{21}$
D. $\frac{a}{b} = \frac{21}{10}$
E. $\frac{a}{b} = \frac{10}{23}$

55) Which of the following lines is parallel to: $6y - 2x = 24$?

A. $y = \frac{1}{3}x + 2$
B. $y = 3x + 5$
C. $y = x - 2$
D. $y = 2x - 1$
E. $y = -x - 1$

56) Sara orders a box of pen for $3 per box. A tax of 8.5% is added to the cost of the pens before a flat shipping fee of $6 closest out the transaction. Which of the following represents total cost of p boxes of pens in dollars?

   A. $1.085(3p) + 6$
   B. $6p + 3$
   C. $1.085(6p) + 3$
   D. $3p + 6$
   E. $6p + 6$

End of Praxis Core Math Practice Test 2

Praxis Core Math (5733) Practice Test 3

2020 - 2021

Total number of questions: 56

Total time: 90 Minutes

You may use a calculator on this practice test.

(On a real Praxis test, there is an onscreen calculator to use.)

1) When a number is subtracted from 24 and the difference is divided by that number, the result is 3. What is the value of the number?
   A. 2
   B. 4
   C. 6
   D. 12
   E. 24

2) An angle is equal to one fifth of its supplement. What is the measure of that angle?
   A. 20
   B. 30
   C. 45
   D. 60
   E. 90

3) In the following figure, point O is the center of the circle and the equilateral triangle has perimeter 45. What is the circumference of the circle? ($\pi = 3$)

   Write your answer in the box below.

   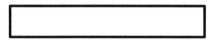

   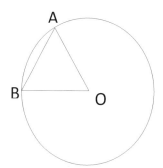

4) If 14% of x is 84 and $\frac{1}{8}$ of y is 18, what is the value of $x - y$?

   Write your answer in the box below.

5) In five successive hours, a car traveled $40\ km, 45\ km, 50\ km, 35\ km$ and $55\ km$. In the next five hours, it traveled with an average speed of $50\ km\ per\ hour$. Find the total distance the car traveled in 10 hours.
   A. $425\ km$
   B. $450\ km$
   C. $475\ km$
   D. $500\ km$
   E. $1,000\ km$

6) How long does a 420–miles trip take moving at 50 miles per hour (*mph*)?

    A. 4 *hours*

    B. 6 *hours and* 24 *minutes*

    C. 8 *hours and* 24 *minutes*

    D. 8 *hours and* 30 *minutes*

    E. 10 *hours and* 30 *minutes*

7) Right triangle ABC has two legs of lengths 6 *cm* (AB) and 8 *cm* (AC). What is the length of the third side (BC)?

    A. 4 *cm*

    B. 6 *cm*

    C. 8 *cm*

    D. 10 *cm*

    E. 20 *cm*

8) The ratio of boys to girls in a school is $2:3$. If there are 600 students in a school, how many boys are in the school.

    A. 540

    B. 360

    C. 300

    D. 280

    E. 240

9) 25 is What percent of 20?

    A. 20%

    B. 25%

    C. 125%

    D. 150%

    E. 300%

10) The perimeter of the trapezoid below is 54. What is its area?

    A. 252 cm^2

    B. 234 cm^2

    C. 216 cm^2

    D. 154 cm^2

    E. 130cm^2

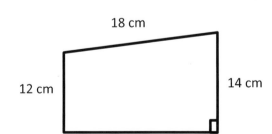

11) Two third of 18 is equal to $\frac{2}{5}$ of what number?
- A. 12
- B. 20
- C. 30
- D. 60
- E. 90

12) The marked price of a computer is D dollar. Its price decreased by 20% in January and later increased by 10% in February. What is the final price of the computer in D dollar?
- A. 0.80 D
- B. 0.88 D
- C. 0.90 D
- D. 1.20 D
- E. 1.40 D

13) The area of a circle is 25 π. What is the circumference of the circle?
- A. 5 π
- B. 10 π
- C. 32 π
- D. 64 π
- E. 124 π

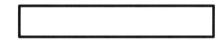

$r = \sqrt{25} = 5$

$C = 2\pi \times 5 = 10$

14) $[6 \times (-24) + 8] - (-4) + [4 \times 5] \div 2 = ?$

Write your answer in the box below.

15) From last year, the price of gasoline has increased from \$1.25 per gallon to \$1.75 per gallon. The new price is what percent of the original price?
- A. 72%
- B. 120%
- C. 140%
- D. 160%
- E. 180%

16) A boat sails 40 miles south and then 30 miles east. How far is the boat from its start point?
   A. 45 *miles*
   B. 50 *miles*
   C. 60 *miles*
   D. 70 *miles*
   E. 80 *miles*

17) Sophia purchased a sofa for $530.40. The sofa is regularly priced at $624. What was the percent discount Sophia received on the sofa?
   A. 12%
   B. 15%
   C. 20%
   D. 25%
   E. 40%

18) The score of Emma was half as that of Ava and the score of Mia was twice that of Ava. If the score of Mia was 60, what is the score of Emma?
   A. 12
   B. 15
   C. 20
   D. 30
   E. 40

19) The average of five consecutive numbers is 38. What is the smallest number?
   A. 38
   B. 36
   C. 34
   D. 12
   E. 8

20) How many tiles of $8 \ cm^2$ is needed to cover a floor of dimension $6 \ cm$ by $24 \ cm$?
   A. 6
   B. 12
   C. 18
   D. 24
   E. 36

21) A rope weighs 600 grams per meter of length. What is the weight in kilograms of 12.2 meters of this rope? ($1 \ kilograms \ = \ 1000 \ grams$)
   A. 0.0732
   B. 0.732
   C. 7.32
   D. 7,320
   E. 73,200

22) A chemical solution contains 4% alcohol. If there is $24\ ml$ of alcohol, what is the volume of the solution?
 A. $240\ ml$
 B. $480\ ml$
 C. $600\ ml$
 D. $1,200\ ml$
 E. $2,400\ ml$

23) The average weight of 18 girls in a class is $60\ kg$ and the average weight of 32 boys in the same class is $62\ kg$. What is the average weight of all the 50 students in that class?
 A. 60
 B. 61.28
 C. 61.68
 D. 61.90
 E. 62.20

24) The price of a laptop is decreased by 10% to $360. What is its original price?
 A. $320
 B. $380
 C. $400
 D. $450
 E. $500

25) The radius of a cylinder is 8 inches and its height is 12 inches. What is the surface area of the cylinder?
 A. $64\ \pi\ in^2$
 B. $128\ \pi\ in^2$
 C. $192\ \pi\ in^2$
 D. $256\ \pi\ in^2$
 E. $320\ \pi\ in^2$

26) The average of $13, 15, 20$ and x is 18. What is the value of x?
 A. 9
 B. 15
 C. 18
 D. 20
 E. 24

27) The price of a sofa is decreased by 25% to $420. What was its original price?
 A. $480
 B. $520
 C. $560
 D. $600
 E. $800

28) A bank is offering 4.5% simple interest on a savings account. If you deposit $8,000, how much interest will you earn in five years?
   A. $360
   B. $720
   C. $1,800
   D. $3,600
   E. $4,800

29) Multiply and write the product in scientific notation:

$$(4.2 \times 10^6) \times (2.6 \times 10^{-5})$$

   A. 1092×10
   B. 10.92×10^6
   C. 109.2×10^{-5}
   D. 10.92×10^{11}
   E. 1.092×10^2

30) If the height of a right pyramid is $12\ cm$ and its base is a square with side $6\ cm$. What is its volume?
   A. $32\ cm^3$
   B. $36\ cm^3$
   C. $48\ cm^3$
   D. $72\ cm^3$
   E. $144\ cm^3$

31) Solve for x: $4(x + 1) = 6(x - 4) + 20$
   A. 12
   B. 8
   C. 6.2
   D. 5.5
   E. 4

32) Which of the following expressions is equivalent to $2x\,(4 + 2y)$?
   A. $2xy + 8x$
   B. $8xy + 8x$
   C. $xy + 8$
   D. $2xy + 8x$
   E. $4xy + 8x$

33) If $y = 4ab + 3b^3$, what is y when $a = 2$ and $b = 3$?
   A. 24
   B. 31
   C. 36
   D. 51
   E. 105

34) The volume of a cube is less than $64\ m^3$. Which of the following can be the cube's side?
   (Select one or more answer choices)
   A. $2\ m$

   B. $3\ m$

   C. $4\ m$

   D. $5\ m$

   E. $6\ m$

$$y = x^2 - 9x + 18$$

35) The equation above represents a quadratic equation in the xy-plane. What is one x-intercepts of the quadratic?

   Write your answer in the box below.

36) A number is chosen at random from 1 to 25. Find the probability of not selecting a composite number.
   A. $\dfrac{9}{25}$
   B. 25
   C. $\dfrac{2}{5}$
   D. 1
   E. 0

37) Which of the following points lies on the line $2x + 4y = 10$
   A. $(2, 1)$
   B. $(-1, 3)$
   C. $(-2, 2)$
   D. $(2, 2)$
   E. $(2, 8)$

38) The price of a car was $20,000 in 2014, $16,000 in 2015 and $12,800 in 2016. What is the rate of depreciation of the price of car per year?
   A. 15%
   B. 20%
   C. 25%
   D. 30%
   E. 50%

39) A ladder leans against a wall forming a $60°$ angle between the ground and the ladder. If the bottom of the ladder is 30 feet away from the wall, how long is the ladder?
   A. $30 \ feet$
   B. $40 \ feet$
   C. $50 \ feet$
   D. $60 \ feet$
   E. $120 \ feet$

40) The area of a circle is less than $81\pi \ ft^2$. Which of the following can be the diameter of the circle? (Select one or more answer choices)
   A. $28ft$

   B. $20ft$

   C. $18ft$

   D. $17ft$

   E. $14ft$

41) If $x + y = 0, \ 4x - 2y = 24$, which of the following ordered pairs (x, y) satisfies both equations?
   A. $(4, 3)$
   B. $(5, 4)$
   C. $(4, -4)$
   D. $(4, -6)$
   E. $(2, -6)$

42) If $f(x) = 3x + 4(x + 1) + 2$ then $f(3x) =$?
   A. $21x + 6$
   B. $16x - 6$
   C. $25x + 4$
   D. $12x + 3$
   E. $2x + 3$

43) A line in the xy-plane passes through origin and has a slope of $\frac{2}{3}$. Which of the following points lies on the line?

   A. $(2,1)$
   B. $(4,1)$
   C. $(9,6)$
   D. $(9,3)$
   E. $(6,-3)$

44) Which of the following is equivalent to $(3n^2 + 4n + 6) - (2n^2 - 5)$?

   A. $n + 4n^2$
   B. $n^2 - 3$
   C. $n^2 + 4n + 11$
   D. $n + 2$
   E. $n - 2$

45) If $(ax + 4)(bx + 3) = 10x^2 + cx + 12$ for all values of x and $a + b = 7$, what are the two possible values for c?

   A. $22, 21$
   B. $20, 22$
   C. $23, 26$
   D. $24, 23$
   E. $24, 26$

46) If $x \neq -4$ and $x \neq 6$, which of the following is equivalent to $\dfrac{1}{\frac{1}{x-6}+\frac{1}{x+4}}$?

   A. $\dfrac{(x-6)(x+4)}{(x-6)+(x+4)}$

   B. $\dfrac{(x+4)+(x-6)}{(x+4)(x-6)}$

   C. $\dfrac{(x+4)(x-6)}{(x+4)-(x+6)}$

   D. $\dfrac{(x+4)+(x-6)}{(x+4)-(x-6)}$

   E. $\dfrac{(x-4)+(x-6)}{(x+4)-(x-6)}$

$$y < a - x \,, y > x + b$$

47) In the xy-plane, if $(0,0)$ is a solution to the system of inequalities above, which of the following relationships between a and b must be true?
   A. $a < b$
   B. $a > b$
   C. $a = b$
   D. $a = b + a$
   E. $a = b - a$

48) Which of the following points lies on the line that goes through the points $(2,4)$ and $(4,5)$?
   A. $(9,9)$
   B. $(9,6)$
   C. $(6,9)$
   D. $(6,6)$
   E. $(0,6)$

49) Calculate $f(4)$ for the following function f.
$$f(x) = x^2 - 3x$$

   A. 0

   B. 4

   C. 12

   D. 20

   E. 24

50) John buys a pepper plant that is 6 inches tall. With regular watering the plant grows 4 inches a year. Writing John's plant's height as a function of time, what does the $y-$intercept represent?
   A. The $y-$intercept represents the rate of grows of the plant which is 4 inches
   B. The $y-$intercept represents the starting height of 6 inches
   C. The $y-$intercept represents the rate of growth of plant which is 4 inches per year
   D. The $y-$intercept is zero
   E. There is no $y-$intercept

51) If $\dfrac{3}{x} = \dfrac{12}{x-9}$ what is the value of $\dfrac{x}{6}$?
   A. -2
   B. 2
   C. $-\dfrac{1}{2}$
   D. $\dfrac{1}{2}$
   E. 0

52) What is the equation of the following graph?

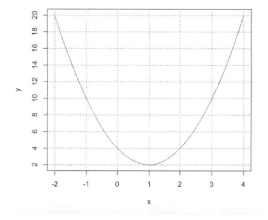

   A. $x^2 + 6x + 5$

   B. $x^2 + 2x + 4$

   C. $2x^2 - 4x + 4$

   D. $2x^2 + 4x + 2$

   E. $4x^2 + 2x + 3$

53) In the $xy-$plane, the line determined by the points $(6, m)$ and $(m, 12)$ passes through the origin. Which of the following could be the value of m?

   A. $\sqrt{6}$

   B. 12

   C. $6\sqrt{2}$

   D. 9

   E. 6

54) A function $g(3) = 5$ and $g(6) = 4$. A function $f(5) = 2$ and $f(4) = 7$. What is the value of $f(g(6))$?

   A. 5

   B. 7

   C. 8

   D. 9

   E. 12

55) What is the area of the following equilateral triangle if the side $AB = 8\ cm$?

   A. $16\sqrt{3}\ cm^2$

   B. $8\sqrt{3}\ cm^2$

   C. $\sqrt{3}\ cm^2$

   D. $8\ cm^2$

   E. $6\ cm^2$

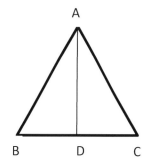

56) Which graph shows a non-proportional linear relationship between x and y?

A.

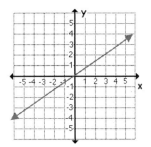

B.

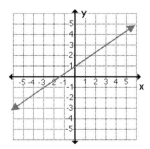

C.

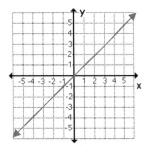

D.

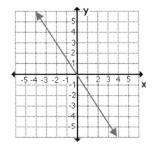

End of Praxis Core Math Practice Test 3

Praxis Core Math (5733) Practice Test 4

2020- 2021

Total number of questions: 56

Total time: 90 Minutes

You may use a calculator on this practice test.

(On a real Praxis test, there is an onscreen calculator to use.)

1) If $f(x) = 3x^3 + 5x^2 + 2x$ and $g(x) = -2$, what is the value of $f(g(x))$?
   A. 36
   B. 32
   C. 24
   D. 8
   E. -8

2) The diagonal of a rectangle is 10 inches long and the height of the rectangle is 8 inches. What is the perimeter of the rectangle?
   A. $10\ inches$
   B. $12\ inches$
   C. $16\ inches$
   D. $18\ inches$
   E. $28\ inches$

3) If $x = \frac{1}{3}$ and $y = \frac{9}{21}$, then which is equal to $\frac{1}{x} \div \frac{y}{3}$?
   A. $\frac{1}{7}$
   B. $\frac{1}{21}$
   C. $\frac{1}{3}$
   D. 9
   E. 21

4) The mean of 50 test scores was calculated as 85. But, it turned out that one of the scores was misread as 94 but it was 69. What is the mean?
   A. 84.5
   B. 87
   C. 87.5
   D. 88.5
   E. 90.5

5) Which of the following answers represents the compound inequality $-4 \le 4x - 8 < 16$?
   A. $-2 \le x \le 8$
   B. $-2 < x \le 8$
   C. $1 < x \le 6$
   D. $1 \le x < 6$
   E. $2 \le x \le 6$

6) A swimming pool holds 2,000 cubic feet of water. The swimming pool is 25 feet long and 10 feet wide. How deep is the swimming pool?
   A. $2\ feet$
   B. $4\ feet$
   C. $6\ feet$
   D. $7\ feet$
   E. $8\ feet$

7) Mr. Carlos family are choosing a menu for their reception. They have 3 choices of appetizers, 7 choices of entrees, 4 choices of cake. How many different menu combinations are possible for them to choose?
   A. 12
   B. 32
   C. 84
   D. 120
   E. 240

8) What is the area of a square whose diagonal is 8?
   A. 16
   B. 32
   C. 36
   D. 64
   E. 124

9) The perimeter of a rectangular yard is 60 meters. What is its length if its width is twice its length?
   A. 10 *meters*
   B. 18 *meters*
   C. 20 *meters*
   D. 24 *meters*
   E. 36 *meters*

10) The average of 6 numbers is 12. The average of 4 of those numbers is 10. What is the average of the other two numbers?
   A. 10
   B. 12
   C. 14
   D. 16
   E. 24

11) The average of five numbers is 24. If a sixth number 42 is added, then, what is the new average?
   A. 25
   B. 26
   C. 27
   D. 28
   E. 36

12) The ratio of boys and girls in a class is 4: 7. If there are 66 students in the class, how many more boys should be enrolled to make the ratio 1: 1?
   A. 8
   B. 10
   C. 12
   D. 18
   E. 28

13) Jason needs an 76% average in his writing class to pass. On his first 4 exams, he earned scores of 68%, 72%, 85%, and 90%. What is the minimum score Jason can earn on his fifth and final test to pass?
   A. 80%,
   B. 70%
   C. 68%
   D. 65%
   E. 60%

14) 5 less than twice a positive integer is 53. What is the integer?
   A. 29
   B. 41
   C. 42
   D. 44
   E. 53

15) A bank is offering 3.5% simple interest on a savings account. If you deposit $12,000, how much interest will you earn in two years?
   A. $420
   B. $840
   C. $4,200
   D. $8,400
   E. $9,600

16) Simplify $6x^2y^3(2x^2y)^3 =$

   A. $12x^4y^6$
   B. $12x^8y^6$
   C. $48x^4y^6$
   D. $48x^8y^6$
   E. $96x^8y^6$

17) The radius of a cylinder is 6 inches and its height is 12 inches. What is the surface area of the cylinder in square inches?

   A. 567.98
   B. 640
   C. 678.24
   D. 888.25
   E. 910.21

18) A cruise line ship left Port A and traveled 80 miles due west and then 150 miles due north. At this point, what is the shortest distance from the cruise to port A?

   A. $70 \ miles$
   B. $80 \ miles$
   C. $150 \ miles$
   D. $230 \ miles$
   E. $170 \ miles$

19) What is the equivalent temperature of $140°F$ in Celsius?

$$C = \frac{5}{9}(F - 32)$$

   A. 32
   B. 40
   C. 48
   D. 52
   E. 60

20) If 150% of a number is 75, then what is the 95% of that number?

   A. 47.5
   B. 50
   C. 70
   D. 85
   E. 90

21) In two successive years, the population of a town is increased by 15% and 20%. What percent of the population is increased after two years?

   A. 32%
   B. 35%
   C. 38%
   D. 68%
   E. 70%

22) Last week 24,000 fans attended a football match. This week three times as many bought tickets, but one sixth of them cancelled their tickets. How many are attending this week?
   A. 48,000
   B. 54,000
   C. 60,000
   D. 72,000
   E. 84,000

23) What is the perimeter of a square that has an area of 64 square inches?
   A. $144\ inches$
   B. $64\ inches$
   C. $56\ inches$
   D. $48\ inches$
   E. $32\ inches$

24) In the xy-plane, the point (4,3) and (3,2) are on line A. Which of the following points could also be on line A?
   A. $(-1,2)$
   B. $(5,7)$
   C. $(3,4)$
   D. $(-1,-2)$
   E. $(-7,-9)$

25) If $f(x) = 2x^3 + 5x^2 + 2x$ and $g(x) = -2$, what is the value of $f(g(x))$?
   A. 36
   B. 32
   C. 24
   D. 4
   E. 0

26) The area of a circle is 64π. What is the diameter of the circle?
   A. 4
   B. 8
   C. 12
   D. 14
   E. 16

27) If a tree casts a 22–foot shadow at the same time that a 3 feet yardstick casts a 2–foot shadow, what is the height of the tree?

   A. $24\ ft$
   B. $28\ ft$
   C. $33\ ft$
   D. $98\ ft$
   E. $108\ ft$

28) Which of the following is equal to the expression below?

$$(4x + 2y)(2x - y)$$

A. $8x^2 - 2y^2$
B. $2x^2 + 6xy - 2y^2$
C. $24x^2 + 2xy - 2y^2$
D. $8x^2 + 2xy - 2y^2$
E. $8x^2 + 2xy - 2y^2$

29) What is the product of all possible values of x in the following equation?

$$|x - 10| = 3$$

A. 3
B. 7
C. 13
D. 91
E. 100

30) What is the slope of a line that is perpendicular to the line $4x - 2y = 12$?

A. -2
B. $-\dfrac{1}{2}$
C. 4
D. 12
E. 14

31) What is the value of the expression $5(x - 2y) + (2 - x)^2$ when $x = 3$ and $y = -2$?

A. -4
B. 20
C. 36
D. 50
E. 80

32) Jason is 15 miles ahead of Joe running at 5.5 miles per hour and Joe is running at the speed of 7 miles per hour. How long does it take Joe to catch Jason?

A. 3 *hours*
B. 4 *hours*
C. 6 *hours*
D. 8 *hours*
E. 10 *hours*

33) 88 students took an exam and 11 of them failed. What percent of the students passed the exam?
   A. 20%
   B. 40.3%
   C. 60%
   D. 87.5%
   E. 90.15

34)   What is the value of y in the following system of equation?

$$3x - 4y = -16$$

$$-x + 2y = 10$$

Write your answer in the box below.

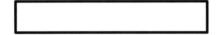

35) If the area of trapezoid is 100, what is the perimeter of the trapezoid?

   A. 25

   B. 35

   C. 45

   D. 55

   E. 65

36) A number is chosen at random from 1 to 25. Find the probability of not selecting a composite number.
   A. $\frac{1}{25}$

   B. 25

   C. $\frac{2}{5}$

   D. 1

   E. 0

37) Removing which of the following numbers will change the average of the numbers to 6?

1, 4, 5, 8, 11, 12

A. 1

B. 4

C. 5

D. 11

E. 12

38) The perimeter of the trapezoid below is 64. What is its area?

Write your answer in the box below.

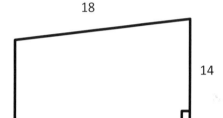

39) If $(x - 2)^2 + 1 > 3x - 1$, then x can equal which of the following?

A. 1

B. 6

C. 8

D. 3

E. 4

40) The volume of cube A is $\frac{1}{2}$ of its surface area. What is the length of an edge of cube A?

Write your answer in the box below.

41) If $\frac{x-3}{5} = N$ and $N = 7$, what is the value of x?

   A. 25
   B. 28
   C. 30
   D. 38
   E. 42

42) Which of the following is equal to $b^{\frac{4}{5}}$?

   A. $\sqrt{b^{\frac{4}{5}}}$
   B. $b^{\frac{4}{5}}$
   C. $\sqrt[5]{b^4}$
   D. $\sqrt[4]{b^5}$
   E. $\sqrt[-4]{b^5}$

43) If function is defined as $f(x) = bx^2 + 15$, and b is a constant and $f(2) = 35$. What is the value of $f(4)$?

   A. 25
   B. 45
   C. 95
   D. 105
   E. 109

44) Find the solution (x, y) to the following system of equations?
$$-3x - y = 6$$
$$6x + 4y = 10$$

   A. $(14, 5)$
   B. $(6, 8)$
   C. $(11, 17)$
   D. $(-\frac{17}{3}, 11)$
   E. $(-6, 11)$

45) Calculate $f(3)$ for the function $f(x) = 3x^2 - 4$.

   A. 23
   B. 30
   C. 48
   D. 50
   E. 60

46) What is the sum of all values of n that satisfies $2n^2 + 16n + 24 = 0$?

A. 8
B. 4
C. -4
D. -8
E. -12

x	$g(x)$
0	3
1	0
2	-3
3	-8
4	-12

$$y = x^2 - 8x + 12$$

47) The equation above represents a parabola in the xy-plane. Which of the following equivalent forms of the equation displays the x-intercepts of the parabola as constants or coefficients?

A. $y = x + 3$

B. $y = x(x - 8)$

C. $y = (x + 6)(x + 2)$

D. $y = (x - 6)(x - 2)$

E. $y = (x - 4)(x - 2)$

48) The function $g(x)$ is defined by a polynomial. Some values of x and $g(x)$ are shown in the table below. Which of the following must be a factor of $g(x)$?

A. x
B. $x + 1$
C. $x - 1$
D. $x + 3$
E. $x - 3$

49) What is the value of $\dfrac{6b}{c}$ when $\dfrac{c}{b} = 2$

A. 6
B. 4
C. 3
D. 1
E. 0

50) Which of the following is equivalent to $\dfrac{x + (5x)^2 + (3x)^3}{x}$?

A. $16x^2 + 25x + 1$
B. $27x^2 + 25x + 1$
C. $16x^2 + 25x$
D. $27x^3 + 16x^2 + 1$
E. $16x^3 - 16x^2 + 1$

51) How many possible outfit combinations come from six shirts, four slacks, and five ties?

Write your answer in the box below

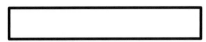

52) The ratio of boys to girls in a school is $2:3$. If there are 500 students in a school, how many boys are in the school.

Write your answer in the box below.

53) What is the solution of the following inequality?

$$|x - 2| \geq 3$$

A. $x \geq 5 \cup x \leq -1$
B. $-1 \leq x \leq 5$
C. $x \geq 5$
D. $x \leq -1$
E. Set of real numbers

54) In the following figure, ABCD is a rectangle. If $a = \sqrt{3}$, and $b = 2a$, find the area of the shaded region. (the shaded region is a trapezoid)

A. 4
B. 2
C. $\sqrt{3}$
D. $2\sqrt{3}$
E. $4\sqrt{3}$

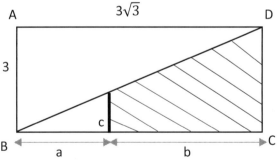

55) On the following figure, what is the area of the quadrilateral $ABCD$?

    A. 22.5
    B. 30
    C. 33.2
    D. 36
    E. 36

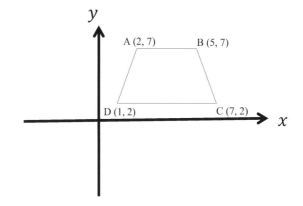

56) If n is an odd integer divisible by 3. Which of the following must be divisible by 2?

    A. $n - 2$
    B. $n + 2$
    C. $2n + 2$
    D. $2n - 1$
    E. $3n - 2$

End of Praxis Core Math Practice Test 4

Praxis Core Math (5733) Practice Test 5

2020- 2021

Total number of questions: 56

Total time: 90 Minutes

You may use a calculator on this practice test.

(On a real Praxis test, there is an onscreen calculator to use.)

1) What is the value of the expression $2(2x - y) + (4 - x)^2$ when $x = 2$ and $y = -1$?
   A. -2
   B. 8
   C. 14
   D. 28
   E. 50

2) A swimming pool holds 1,500 cubic feet of water. The swimming pool is 15 feet long and 10 feet wide. How deep is the swimming pool?
   A. $2\ feet$
   B. $4\ feet$
   C. $6\ feet$
   D. $8\ feet$
   E. $10\ feet$

3) Mr. Carlos family are choosing a menu for their reception. They have 5 choices of appetizers, 4 choices of entrees, 3 choices of cake. How many different menu combinations are possible for them to choose?
   A. 12
   B. 32
   C. 60
   D. 120
   E. 240

4) If $f(x) = x^3 - 2x^2 + 8x$ and $g(x) = 3$, what is the value of $f(g(x))$?
   A. -3
   B. 11
   C. 22
   D. 23
   E. 33

5) The diagonal of a rectangle is 10 $inches$ long and the height of the rectangle is 8 $inches$. What is the perimeter of the rectangle?
   A. $10\ inches$
   B. $12\ inches$
   C. $16\ inches$
   D. $18\ inches$
   E. $28\ inches$

6) Which of the following could be the product of two consecutive prime numbers? (Select one or more answer choices)

A. 2

B. 10

C. 14

D. 15

E. 35

7) The average of seven numbers is 32. If an eighth number 18 is added, then, what is the new average?
   A. 24
   B. 28
   C. 30.25
   D. 32
   E. 34

8) The ratio of boys and girls in a class is $4:7$. If there are 44 students in the class, how many more boys should be enrolled to make the ratio $1:1$?
   A. 8
   B. 10
   C. 12
   D. 14
   E. 28

9) What is the value of x in the following equation? $\frac{2}{3}x + \frac{1}{6} = \frac{1}{3}$
   A. 6
   B. $\frac{1}{2}$
   C. $\frac{1}{3}$
   D. $\frac{1}{4}$
   E. $\frac{1}{12}$

10) A bank is offering 2.5% simple interest on a savings account. If you deposit $16,000, how much interest will you earn in three years?
   A. $610
   B. $1,200
   C. $2,400
   D. $4,800
   E. $6,400

11) Jason needs an 75% average in his writing class to pass. On his first 4 exams, he earned scores of 68%, 72%, 85%, and 90%. What is the minimum score Jason can earn on his fifth and final test to pass?
   A. 80%
   B. 70%
   C. 68%
   D. 64%
   E. 60%

12) Two dice are thrown simultaneously, what is the probability of getting a sum of 6 or 9?
   A. $\dfrac{1}{3}$
   B. $\dfrac{1}{12}$
   C. $\dfrac{1}{6}$
   D. $\dfrac{1}{4}$
   E. $\dfrac{1}{36}$

13) If $2y + 6 < 30$, then y could be equal to? (Select one or more answer choices)
   A. 15

   B. 14

   C. 12

   D. 8

   E. -12

14) Which of the following is equal to the expression below?
$$(3x - y)(2x + 2y)$$
   A. $6x^2 - 2y^2$
   B. $6x^2 + 4xy + 2y^2$
   C. $12x^2 + 6xy + 2y^2$
   D. $6x^2 + 4xy - 2y^2$
   E. $4x^2 + 6xy - 2y^2$

15) What is the product of all possible values of x in the following equation?

$$|x - 12| = 4$$

    A. 4
    B. 8
    C. 16
    D. 128
    E. 200

16) What is the slope of a line that is perpendicular to the line $4x - 2y = 12$?

    A. -2
    B. $-\frac{1}{2}$
    C. 4
    D. 12
    E. 14

17) Last week 18,000 fans attended a football match. This week three times as many bought tickets, but one sixth of them cancelled their tickets. How many are attending this week?

    A. 42,000
    B. 54,000
    C. 45,000
    D. 65,000
    E. 78,000

18) What is the perimeter of a square that has an area of 81 square inches?

    A. $129\ inches$
    B. $72\ inches$
    C. $68\ inches$
    D. $58\ inches$
    E. $36\ inches$

19) What are the zeros of the function: $f(x) = x^2 - 7x + 12$?

    A. 0
    B. $-2, -3$
    C. $0, 4, 3$
    D. $-4, -3$
    E. $4, 3$

20) The mean of 50 test scores was calculated as 88. But, it turned out that one of the scores was misread as 94 but it was 69. What is the mean?

    A. 85
    B. 87
    C. 87.5
    D. 88.5
    E. 90.5

21) What is the equivalent temperature of $122°F$ in Celsius?

$$C = \frac{5}{9}(F - 32)$$

   A. 22
   B. 50
   C. 58
   D. 62
   E. 84

22) The perimeter of a rectangular *yard* is 120 *meters*. What is its length if its width is twice its length?

   A. 20 *meters*
   B. 22 *meters*
   C. 24 *meters*
   D. 28 *meters*
   E. 30 *meters*

23) If 150% of a number is 75, then what is the 90% of that number?

   A. 45
   B. 50
   C. 70
   D. 85
   E. 90

24) What is the slope of the line: $8x - 4y = 8$?

   A. -1
   B. -2
   C. 1
   D. 1.5
   E. 2

25) In two successive years, the population of a town is increased by 12% and 25%. What percent of the population is increased after two years?

   A. 34%
   B. 38%
   C. 40%
   D. 60%
   E. 80%

26) The average of 8 numbers is 14. The average of 6 of those numbers is 12. What is the average of the other two numbers?

   A. 12
   B. 14
   C. 16
   D. 20
   E. 28

27) Five years ago, Amy was three times as old as Mike was. If Mike is 10 years old now, how old is Amy?

    A. 4
    B. 8
    C. 12
    D. 14
    E. 20

28) If a tree casts a 18–foot shadow at the same time that a 4 feet yardstick casts a 3–foot shadow, what is the height of the tree?

    A. 18 ft
    B. 20 ft
    C. 24 ft
    D. 54 ft
    E. 62 ft

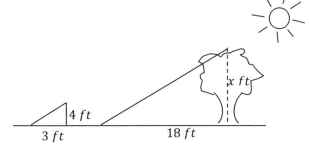

29) x is $y\%$ of what number?

    A. $\dfrac{100x}{y}$

    B. $\dfrac{100y}{x}$

    C. $\dfrac{x}{100y}$

    D. $\dfrac{y}{100x}$

    E. $\dfrac{xy}{100}$

30) What is the value of expression? $-15 + 6 \times (-5) - [4 + 22 \times (-4)] \div 2 = ?$

    Write your answer in the box below.

31) 6 liters of water are poured into an aquarium that's 15cm long, 5cm wide, and 60cm high. How many cm will the water level in the aquarium rise due to this added water? (1 liter of water = 1000 cm3)

A. 80

B. 40

C. 20

D. 10

E. 5

32) If a box contains red and blue balls in ratio of 2 : 3, how many red balls are there if 90 blue balls are in the box?

A. 90

B. 60

C. 30

D. 10

E. 8

33) If $|a| < 1$, then which of the following is true? ($b > 0$)?

    I. $-b < ba < b$

    II. $-a < a^2 < a$ $if \ a < 0$

    III. $-5 < 2a - 3 < -1$

A. I only

B. II only

C. I and III only

D. III only

E. I, II and III

34) A cruise line ship left Port A and traveled 80 miles due west and then 150 miles due north. At this point, what is the shortest distance from the cruise to port A?

A. 70 $miles$

B. 80 $miles$

C. 150 $miles$

D. 230 $miles$

E. 170 $miles$

35) If 30% of a number is 12, what is the number?

A. 12

B. 25

C. 40

D. 45

E. 50

36) Jason is 15 miles ahead of Joe running at 4.5 miles per hour and Joe is running at the speed of 7 miles per hour. How long does it take Joe to catch Jason?

A. $3\ hours$

B. $4\ hours$

C. $6\ hours$

D. $8\ hours$

E. $10\ hours$

37) 55 Students took an exam and 11 of them failed. What percent of the students passed the exam?

A. 20%

B. 40%

C. 60%

D. 80%

E. 90%

38) The following table represents the value of x and function $f(x)$. Which of the following could be the equation of the function $f(x)$?

A. $f(x) = x^2 - 5$

B. $f(x) = x^2 - 1$

C. $f(x) = \sqrt{x+2}$

D. $f(x) = \sqrt{x} + 4$

D. $f(x) = \sqrt{x+1} + 4$

x	$f(x)$
1	5
4	6
9	7
16	8

39) In the following equation when z is divided by 3, what is the effect on x?

$$x = \frac{8y + \dfrac{r}{r+1}}{\dfrac{6}{z}}$$

A. x is divided by 2

B. x is divided by 3

C. x does not change

D. x is multiplied by 3

E. x is multiplied by 2

40) Michelle and Alec can finish a job together in 200 minutes. If Michelle can do the job by herself in 5 hours, how many minutes does it take Alec to finish the job?

Write your answer in the box below.

╔══════════════════╗
║   ║
╚══════════════════╝

41) If x is a real number, and if $x^3 + 18 = 130$, then x lies between which two consecutive integers?
   A. 1 and 2
   B. 2 and 3
   C. 3 and 4
   D. 4 and 5
   E. 5 and 6

42) If $\frac{3x}{25} = \frac{x-1}{5}$, $x =$
   A. $\frac{1}{5}$

   B. $\frac{5}{2}$

   C. 3

   D. 5

   E. 8

43) If $(x - 2)^3 = 27$ which of the following could be the value of $(x - 6)(x - 4)$?
   A. 1
   B. 2
   C. 6
   D. -1
   E. -2

44) What is the value of y in the following system of equation?

$$3x - 4y = -20$$

$$-x + 2y = 10$$

Write your answer in the box below.

╔══════════════════╗
║   ║
╚══════════════════╝

45) If function is defined as $f(x) = bx^2 + 15$, and b is a constant and $f(2) = 35$. What is the value of $f(3)$?

    A. 25
    B. 45
    C. 60
    D. 105
    E. 115

46) Calculate $f(3)$ for the function $f(x) = 3x^2 - 5$.

    A. 22
    B. 30
    C. 48
    D. 50
    E. 60

47) What are the zeroes of the function $f(x) = x^3 + 8x^2 + 12x$?

    A. 2
    B. 6
    C. $0, 2, 6$
    D. $0, -2, -6$
    E. $0, -2, 6$

48) If the area of the following rectangular $ABCD$ is 100, and E is the midpoint of AB, what is the area of the shaded part

    A. 25
    B. 45
    C. 50
    D. 80
    E. 90

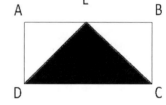

$$y = x^2 - 9x + 14$$

49) The equation above represents a parabola in the xy-plane. Which of the following equivalent forms of the equation displays the x-intercepts of the parabola as constants or coefficients?

    A. $y = x + 2$

    B. $y = x(x - 7)$

    C. $y = (x + 2)(x + 7)$

    D. $y = (x - 2)(x - 7)$

    E. $y = (x - 1)(x - 7)$

50) The function $g(x)$ is defined by a polynomial. Some values of x and $g(x)$ are shown in the table below. Which of the following must be a factor of $g(x)$?

A. $x - 2$
B. $x - 1$
C. $x + 2$
D. $x + 1$
E. $x + 3$

x	$g(x)$
-1	4
-2	0
0	5
1	4
2	6

51) What is the value of $\frac{8b}{c}$ when $\frac{c}{b} = 2$

A. 6
B. 5
C. 4
D. 1
E. 0

52) $\dfrac{1\frac{4}{3} + \frac{1}{4}}{2\frac{1}{2} - \frac{17}{8}}$ is approximately equal to

A. 5.88
B. 6.88
C. 9
D. 12
E. 16

53) Which of the following lines is parallel to: $y - 2x = 36$?

A. $y = 2x + 2$
B. $y = 3x + 5$
C. $y = x - 2$
D. $y = \frac{1}{3}x - 1$
E. $y = -x - 1$

54) When 40% of 60 is added to 12% of 600, the resulting number is:

A. 24
B. 72
C. 96
D. 140
E. 180

55) What is the solution of the following inequality?

$$|x - 2| \geq 4$$

A. $x \geq 6 \cup x \leq -2$
B. $-2 \leq x \leq 6$
C. $x \geq 6$
D. $x \leq -2$
E. $x \leq 2$

56) Which of the following expressions is equal to $\sqrt{\dfrac{x^2}{2} + \dfrac{x^2}{16}}$?

A. x

B. $\dfrac{3x}{4}$

C. $x\sqrt{x}$

D. $\dfrac{x\sqrt{x}}{4}$

E. $\dfrac{x\sqrt{x}}{2}$

End of Praxis Core Math Practice Test 5

Praxis Core Math Practice Tests Answer Keys

Now, it's time to review your results to see where you went wrong and what areas you need to improve.

Praxis Core Math Practice Test 1						Praxis Core Math Practice Test 2					
1	C	21	D	41	C	1	C	21	E	41	D
2	B	22	C	42	A	2	D	22	E	42	C
3	D	23	C	43	C	3	D	23	B	43	B
4	D	24	D	44	C	4	D	24	A	44	D,E
5	E	25	A	45	C	5	B	25	D	45	28
6	E	26	C	46	A	6	C	26	A	46	D
7	E	27	B	47	B	7	E	27	E	47	A
8	D	28	C	48	D	8	C	28	B	48	D
9	E	29	-64	49	B	9	B	29	C	49	-30
10	C	30	2.5	50	C	10	D	30	D	50	D,E
11	B	31	B	51	97.6	11	B	31	C	51	C
12	10	32	B	52	8	12	E	32	C	52	C
13	1.75	33	B	53	C	13	C	33	D	53	B
14	45	34	D	54	B	14	E	34	E	54	B
15	B	35	C	55	A	15	B	35	E	55	A
16	B	36	E	56	C	16	B	36	B	56	A
17	A	37	E	57		17	D	37	E	57	
18	E	38	A	58		18	C	38	D	58	
19	B	39	D	59		19	C	39	C	59	
20	A	40	A	60		20	E	40	A	60	

Praxis Core Math Practice Test 3						Praxis Core Math Practice Test 4					
1	C	21	C	41	C	1	E	21	C	41	D
2	B	22	C	42	A	2	E	22	C	42	C
3	90	23	B	43	C	3	E	23	E	43	C
4	456	24	C	44	C	4	A	24	D	44	D
5	C	25	E	45	C	5	D	25	E	45	A
6	C	26	E	46	A	6	E	26	E	46	D
7	D	27	C	47	B	7	C	27	C	47	D
8	E	28	C	48	D	8	B	28	A	48	C
9	C	29	E	49	B	9	A	29	D	49	C
10	E	30	E	50	B	10	D	30	B	50	B
11	C	31	E	51	C	11	C	31	C	51	120
12	B	32	E	52	C	12	D	32	E	52	200
13	B	33	E	53	C	13	D	33	D	53	A
14	-122	34	A, B	54	B	14	A	34	7	54	E
15	C	35	3, 6	55	A	15	B	35	B	55	A
16	B	36	C	56	B	16	D	36	C	56	C
17	B	37	B			17	C	37	D		
18	B	38	B			18	E	38	260		
19	B	39	D			19	E	39	C		
20	C	40	D,E			20	A	40	3		

Praxis Core Math Practice Test 5

1	C	21	B	41	D
2	E	22	A	42	B
3	C	23	A	43	D
4	E	24	E	44	5
5	E	25	C	45	C
6	D,E	26	D	46	A
7	C	27	E	47	D
8	C	28	C	48	C
9	D	29	A	49	D
10	B	30	-3	50	C
11	E	31	A	51	C
12	D	32	B	52	B
13	D,E	33	C	53	A
14	D	34	E	54	C
15	D	35	C	55	A
16	B	36	C	56	B
17	C	37	D		
18	E	38	D		
19	E	39	B		
20	C	40	600		

Praxis Core Math Practice Tests Answers and Explanations

Praxis Core Math Practice Test 1

1) Choice C is correct

Add the first 5 numbers. $40 + 45 + 50 + 35 + 55 = 225$, To find the distance traveled in the next 5 hours, multiply the average by number of hours. $Distance = Average \times Rate = 65 \times 5 = 325$. Add both numbers. $325 + 225 = 550$

2) Choice B is correct

Use distance formula: $Distance = Rate \times time \Rightarrow 420 = 65 \times T$, divide both sides by $65. 420 \div 65 = T \Rightarrow T = 6.4 \; hours.$ Change hours to minutes for the decimal part. $0.4 \; hours = 0.4 \times 60 = 24 \; minutes.$

3) Choice D is correct

Use Pythagorean Theorem: $a^2 + b^2 = c^2 \Rightarrow 5^2 + 12^2 = c^2 \Rightarrow 169 = c^2 \Rightarrow c = 13$

4) Choice D is correct

Of the 30 employees, there are 5 females under age 45 and 6 males age 45 or older. Therefore, the probability that the person selected will be either a female under age 45 or a male age 45 or older is: $\frac{5}{30} + \frac{6}{30} = \frac{11}{30}$

5) Choice E is correct

Use FOIL (First, Out, In, Last).$(7x + 2y)(5x + 2y) = 35x^2 + 14xy + 10xy + 4y^2 =$

$$35x^2 + 24xy + 4y^2$$

6) Choice E is correct

Use distributive property: $5x(4 + 2y) = 20x + 10xy$

7) Choice E is correct

$y = 5ab + 3b^3$. Plug in the values of a and b in the equation: $a = 2$ and $b = 3$.

$y = 5(2)(3) + 3(3)^3 = 30 + 3(27) = 30 + 81 = 111$

8) Choice D is correct

x and z are colinear. y and $5x$ are colinear. Therefore,

$x + z = y + 5x, subtract \; x \; from \; both \; sides, then, z = y + 4x$

9) Choice E is correct

The perimeter of the trapezoid is 64. Therefore, the missing side (height) is

$= 64 - 18 - 12 - 14 = 20$. Area of the trapezoid: $A = \frac{1}{2} h (b_1 + b_2) =$

$$\frac{1}{2} (20) (12 + 14) = 260$$

10) Choice C is correct

Let x be the number. Write the equation and solve for x. $\frac{2}{3} \times 15 = \frac{2}{5} \cdot x \Rightarrow \frac{2 \times 15}{3} = \frac{2x}{5}$, use

cross multiplication to solve for x. $5 \times 30 = 2x \times 3 \Rightarrow 150 = 6x \Rightarrow x = 25$

11) Choice B is correct

To find the discount, multiply the number by $(100\% - rate\ of\ discount)$. Therefore, for the first discount we get: $(D) (100\% - 25\%) = (D)(0.75) = 0.75$. For increase of 10%: $(0.75\ D)(100\% + 10\%) = (0.75\ D)(1.10) = 0.82\ D = 82\%\ of\ D$ or $0.82\ D$.

12) The answer is 10

$\frac{y}{5} = x - \frac{2}{5}x + 2$, Multiply both sides of the equation by 5. Then: $5 \times \frac{y}{5} = 5 \times \left(x - \frac{2}{5}x + 2\right) \rightarrow$
$y = 5x - 2x + 10 \rightarrow y = 3x + 10$, now, subtract $3x$ from both sides of the equation. Then:

$y - 3x = 10$

13) The answer is 1.75

First, factorize the numerator and simplify. $\frac{x^2 - 16}{x+4} + 3(x + 4) = 15 \rightarrow \frac{(x-4)(x+4)}{x+4} + 3x + 12 = 15$

Divide both sides of the fraction by $(x + 4)$. Then: $x - 4 + 3x + 12 = 15 \rightarrow 4x + 8 = 15$

Subtract 8 from both sides of the equation. Then: $\rightarrow 4x = 15 - 8 = 7 \rightarrow x = \frac{7}{4}$ or $x = 1.75$

14) The answer is 45

Let L be the length of the rectangular and W be the with of the rectangular. Then,

$L = 4W + 3$, The perimeter of the rectangle is 36 meters. Therefore:

$2L + 2W = 36$, $L + W = 18$, Replace the value of L from the first equation into the second equation and solve for W: $(4W + 3) + W = 18 \rightarrow 5W + 3 = 18 \rightarrow 5W = 15 \rightarrow W = 3$

The width of the rectangle is 3 meters and its length is: $L = 4W + 3 = 4(3) + 3 = 15$

The area of the rectangle is: $length \times width = 3 \times 15 = 45$

15) Choice B is correct

Use the formula of areas of circles. $Area = \pi r^2 \Rightarrow 49\pi = \pi r^2 \Rightarrow 49 = r^2 \Rightarrow r = 7$

Radius of the circle is 7. Now, use the circumference formula: Circumference =

$$2\pi r = 2\pi\,(7) = 14\,\pi$$

16) Choice B is correct

Use the formula for Percent of Change. $\frac{New\ Value - Old\ Value}{Old\ Value} \times 100\%$.

$\frac{28-50}{50} \times 100\ \% = -44\%$ (negative sign here means that the new price is less than old price).

17) Choice A is correct

Let x be the number of years. Therefore, \$2,000 per year equals $2000x$. starting from \$26,000 annual salary means you should add that amount to $2000x$. Income more than that is:

$I > 2000\,x\ +\ 26000$

18) Choice E is correct

Use the information provided in the question to draw the shape.

Use Pythagorean Theorem: $a^2 + b^2 = c^2$

$60^2 + 80^2 = c^2 \Rightarrow 3600 + 6400 = c^2 \Rightarrow 10000 = c^2 \Rightarrow c = 100$

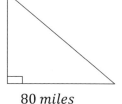

60 *miles*

80 *miles*

19) Choice B is correct

The question is this: 530.40 is what percent of 631?

$percent = \frac{530.40}{631} = 84.05 \cong 84$. 530.40 is 84% of 631. Therefore, the discount is:

$100\% - 84\% = 16\%$

20) Choice A is correct

If the score of Mia was 40, therefore the score of Ava is 20. Since, the score of Emma was half as that of Ava, therefore, the score of Emma is 10.

21) Choice D is correct

If 17 balls are removed from the bag at random, there will be one ball in the bag. The probability of choosing a brown ball is 1 out of 18. Therefore, the probability of not choosing a brown ball is 17 out of 18 and the probability of having not a brown ball after removing 17 balls is the same.

22) Choice C is correct

Let x be the smallest number. Then, these are the numbers: $x, x + 1, x + 2, x + 3, x + 4$

$$\text{average} = \frac{\text{sum of terms}}{\text{number of terms}} \Rightarrow 36 = \frac{x+(x+1)+(x+2)+(x+3)+(x+4)}{5} \Rightarrow 36 = \frac{5x+10}{5} \Rightarrow$$

$$180 = 5x + 10 \Rightarrow 170 = 5x \Rightarrow x = 34$$

23) Choice C is correct

Use this formula: Percent of Change: $\dfrac{\text{New Value} - \text{Old Value}}{Old\ Value} \times 100\%$.

$\dfrac{18,200 - 28,000}{28,000} \times 100\% = -35\%$. The negative sign means that the price decreased

24) Choice D is correct

If the length of the box is 36, then the width of the box is one third of it, 12, and the height of the box is 4 (one third of the width). The volume of the box is: $V = lwh = (36)(12)(4) = 1,728$

25) Choice A is correct

Write a proportion and solve for the missing number. $\dfrac{32}{12} = \dfrac{6}{x} \rightarrow 32x = 6 \times 12 = 72$

$32x = 72 \rightarrow x = \dfrac{72}{32} = 2.25$

26) Choice C is correct

Let x be the number. Write the equation and solve for x. $(28 - x) \div x = 3$

Multiply both sides by x. $(28 - x) = 3x$, then add x both sides. $28 = 4x$, now divide both sides by 4. $x = 7$

27) Choice B is correct

The sum of supplement angles is 180. Let x be that angle. Therefore, $x + 9x = 180$

$10x = 180$, divide both sides by 10: $x = 18$

28) Choice C is correct

The average speed of john is: $150 \div 6 = 25$, The average speed of Alice is: $140 \div 4 = 35$

Write the ratio and simplify. $25 : 35 \Rightarrow 5 : 7$

29) The answer is: -64

Use PEMDAS (order of operation): $[3 \times (-14) - 48] - 14 + [3 \times 8] \div 2 =$

$$[-42 - 48] + 14 + 24 \div 2 = -90 + 14 + 12 = -64$$

30) The answer is 2.5

First, use distribute property to simplify $-4(x + 2)$. $-4(x + 2) = -4x - 8$

Now, combine like terms: $x - 4(x + 2) = -15.5 \rightarrow x - 4x - 8 = -15.5 \rightarrow -3x - 8 = -15.5$

Add 8 to both sides of the equation: $-3x - 8 + 8 = -15.5 + 8 \rightarrow -3x = -7.5$. Divide both sides by -3. Then: $-3x = -7.5 \rightarrow \frac{-3x}{-3} = \frac{-7.5}{-3} \rightarrow x = 2.5$

31) Choice B is correct

$average \ (mean) = \frac{sum \ of \ terms}{number \ of \ terms} = \frac{8+11+14+16+19.5+16+14.5}{7} = 14.14$

32) Choice B is correct

6% of the volume of the solution is alcohol. Let x be the volume of the solution.

Then: $6\% \ of \ x = 24 \ ml \Rightarrow 0.06 \ x = 24 \Rightarrow x = 24 \div 0.06 = 400$

33) Choice B is correct

$average = \frac{sum \ of \ terms}{number \ of \ terms}$. The sum of the weight of all girls is: $18 \times 56 = 1,008 \ kg$

The sum of the weight of all boys is: $32 \times 62 = 1,984 \ kg$. The sum of the weight of all students is: $1,008 + 1,984 = 2,992 \ kg$. $average = \frac{2992}{50} = 59.84$

34) Choice D is correct

Let x be the original price. If the price of a laptop is decreased by 20% to $360, then: $80\% \ of$

$x = 360 \Rightarrow 0.80x = 360 \Rightarrow x = 360 \div 0.80 = 450$

35) Choice C is correct

Use simple interest formula: $I = prt$. (I = interest, p = principal, r = rate, t = time). $I = (9,000)(0.045)(5) = 2,025$

36) Choice E is correct

$(2.9 \times 10^6) \times (2.6 \times 10^{-5}) = (2.9 \times 2.6) \times (10^6 \times 10^{-5}) = 7.54 \times (10^{6+(-5)})$
$= 7.54 \times 10^1$

37) Choice E is correct

The formula of the volume of pyramid is: $V = \frac{l \times w \times h}{3}$

The length and width of the pyramid is $6 \ cm$ and its height is $14 \ cm$. Therefore:

$V = \frac{6 \times 6 \times 14}{3} = 168 \ cm^3$

38) Choice A is correct

Let x be the integer. Then: $2x - 5 = 73$, Add 5 both sides: $2x = 78$, Divide both sides by 2:

$$x = 39$$

39) Choice D is correct

To find the discount, multiply the number by $(100\% - ate\ of\ discount)$. Therefore, for the first discount we get: $(300)\ (100\% - 15\%) = (300)\ (0.85)$. For the next 15% discount: $(300)\ (0.85)\ (0.85)$.

40) Choice A is correct

Plug in each pair of number in the equation: $2x + 4y = 8$

A. $(2, 1)$: $2\ (2) + 4\ (1) = 8$
B. $(-1, 3)$: $2\ (-1) + \ 4\ (3) = 10$
C. $(-2, 2)$: $2\ (-2) + \ 4\ (2) = 4$
D. $(2, 2)$: $2\ (2) + 4\ (2) = 12$
E. $(2, 8)$: $2\ (2) + 4\ (8) = 36$

Only choice A is correct.

41) Choice C is correct

Plugin the values of x and y provided in the choices into both equations. Let's start with $2x + 2y = 2$:

A. $(1, 3)$ $2x + 2y = 2 \rightarrow 2 + 6 \neq 2$
B. $(2, 4)$ $2x + y = 2 \rightarrow 4 + 8 \neq 2$
C. $(2, -1)$ $2x + 2y = 2 \rightarrow 4 + (-2) = 2$
D. $(4, -6)$ $2x + 2y = 2 \rightarrow 12 + (-12) \neq 2$
E. $(1, -6)$ $2x + 2y = 2 \rightarrow 2 + (-12) \neq 2$

Only choice C is correct.

42) Choice A is correct

If $f(x) = 3x + 4(x + 1) + 2$, then find $f(4x)$ by substituting $4x$ for every x in the function. This gives: $f(4x) = 3\ (4x) + \ 4(4x + 1) + 2$

It simplifies to: $f(4x) = 3\ (4x) + 4(4x + 1) + 2 = 12x + 16x + 4 + 2 = 28x + 6$

43) Choice C is correct

First, find the equation of the line. All lines through the origin are of the form $y = mx$, so the equation is $y = \frac{1}{3}x$. Of the given choices, only choice C $(9,3)$, satisfies this equation:

$$y = \frac{1}{3}x \rightarrow 3 = \frac{1}{3}(9) = 3$$

44) Choice C is correct

$(3n^2 + 2n + 6) - (2n^2 - 4)$. Add like terms together: $3n^2 - 2n^2 = n^2$, $2n$ doesn't have like terms. $6 - (-4) = 10$, Combine these terms into one expression to find the answer:

$$n^2 + 2n + 10$$

45) Choice C is correct

Simplify and solve for x in the equation. $4(x + 1) = 6(x - 4) + 20$, $4x + 4 = 6x - 24 + 20$, $4x + 4 = 6x - 4$. Subtract $4x$ from both sides: $4 = 2x - 4$, Add 4 to both sides: $8 = 2x$, $4 = x$

46) Choice A is correct

To rewrite $\dfrac{1}{\frac{1}{x-5}+\frac{1}{x+4}}$, first simplify $\dfrac{1}{x-5} + \dfrac{1}{x+4}$.

$$\frac{1}{x-5} + \frac{1}{x+4} = \frac{1(x+4)}{(x-5)(x+4)} + \frac{1(x-5)}{(x+4)(x-5)} = \frac{(x+4)+(x-5)}{(x+4)(x-5)}$$

Then: $\dfrac{1}{\frac{1}{x-5}+\frac{1}{x+4}} = \dfrac{1}{\frac{(x+4)+(x-5)}{(x+4)(x-5)}} = \dfrac{(x-5)(x+4)}{(x-5)+(x+4)}$. (Remember, $\dfrac{1}{\frac{1}{x}} = x$)

This result is equivalent to the expression in choice A.

47) Choice B is correct

Since $(0, 0)$ is a solution to the system of inequalities, substituting 0 for x and 0 for y in the given system must result in two true inequalities. After this substitution, $y < c - x$ becomes $0 < a$, and $y > x + b$ becomes $0 > b$. Hence, a is positive and b is negative. Therefore, $c > b$.

48) Choice D is correct

$3x + 10 = 46 \rightarrow 3x = 46 - 10 = 36 \rightarrow x = \dfrac{36}{3} = 12$

49) Choice B is correct

The input value is 5. Then: $x = 5$. $f(x) = x^2 - 3x \rightarrow f(5) = 5^2 - 3(5) = 25 - 15 = 10$

50) Choice C is correct

Multiplying each side of $\dfrac{4}{x} = \dfrac{12}{x-8}$ by $x(x - 8)$ gives $4(x - 8) = 12(x)$, distributing the 4 over the values within the parentheses yields $x - 8 = 3x$ or $x = -4$.

Therefore, the value of $\dfrac{x}{2} = \dfrac{-4}{2} = -2$.

51) The answer is 97.6

The area of the square is 595.36. Therefore, the side of the square is square root of the area.

$\sqrt{595.36} = 24.4$.   Four times the side of the square is the perimeter: $4 \times 24.4 = 97.6$

52) The answer is 8

Use formula of rectangle prism volume. $V = (length)(width)(height) \Rightarrow$

$2000 = (25)(10)(height) \Rightarrow height = 2,000 \div 250 = 8$

53) Choice C is correct

Let x be all expenses, then $\frac{22}{100}x = \$660 \rightarrow x = \frac{100 \times \$660}{22} = \$3,000$

Mr. Jones spent for his rent: $\frac{27}{100} \times \$3,000 = \$810$

54) Choice B is correct

It is given that $g(5) = 4$. Therefore, to find the value of $f(g(5))$, then $f(g(5)) = f(4) = 6$

55) Choice A is correct

Area of the triangle is: $\frac{1}{2}AD \times BC$ and AD is perpendicular to BC. Triangle ADC is a

$30° - 60° - 90°$ right triangle. The relationship among all sides of right triangle $30° - 60° - 90°$ is provided in the following triangle: In this triangle, the opposite side of $30°$ angle is half of the hypotenuse. And the opposite side of $60°$ is opposite of $30° \times \sqrt{3}$

$CD = 6$, then $AD = 6 \times \sqrt{3}$

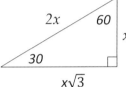

Area of the triangle ABC is: $\frac{1}{2}AD \times BC = \frac{1}{2}6\sqrt{3} \times 12 = 36\sqrt{3}$

56) Choice C is correct

$6 \blacksquare 28 = \sqrt{6^2 + 28} = \sqrt{36 + 28} = \sqrt{64} = 8$

Praxis Core Math Practice Test 2

1) Choice C is correct

$average\ (mean) = \frac{\text{sum of terms}}{\text{number of terms}} \Rightarrow 90 = \frac{sum\ of\ terms}{50} \Rightarrow sum = 90 \times 50 = 4500$

The difference of 94 and 69 is 25. Therefore, 25 should be subtracted from the sum.

$4500 - 25 = 4475,\ mean = \frac{\text{sum of terms}}{\text{number of terms}} \Rightarrow mean = \frac{4475}{50} = 89.5$

2) Choice D is correct

For sum of 5: $(1\ \&\ 4)\ and\ (4\ \&\ 1), (2\ \&\ 3)$ and $(3\ \&\ 2)$, therefore we have 4 options.
For sum of 8: $(5\ \&\ 3)and\ (3\ \&\ 5), (4\ \&\ 4)$ and $(2\ \&\ 6)$, and $(6\ \&\ 2)$,we have 5 options. To get a sum of 5 or 8 for two dice: $4 + 5 = 9$.Since, we have $6 \times 6 = 36$ total number of options, the probability of getting a sum of 5 and 8 is 9 out of 36 or $\frac{9}{36} = \frac{1}{4}$

3) Choice D is correct

Use FOIL method. $(5x + 2y)(2x - y) = 10x^2 - 5xy + 4xy - 2y^2 = 10x^2 - xy - 2y^2$

4) Choice D is correct

To solve absolute values equations, write two equations. $x - 10$ could be positive 4, or negative 4. Therefore, $x - 10 = 4 \Rightarrow x = 14$, $x - 10 = -4 \Rightarrow x = 6$. Find the product of solutions: $6 \times 14 = 84$

5) Choice B is correct

The equation of a line in slope intercept form is: $y = \mathrm{m}x + b$. Solve for y.

$4x - 2y = 6 \Rightarrow -2y = 6 - 4x \Rightarrow y = (6 - 4x) \div (-2) \Rightarrow y = 2x - 3$. The slope is 2.

The slope of the line perpendicular to this line is: $m_1 \times m_2 = -1 \Rightarrow 2 \times m_2 = -1 \Rightarrow m_2 = -\frac{1}{2}$.

6) Choice C is correct

Plug in the value of x and y. $x = 3$ and $y = -2$.

$6(x - 2y) + (2 - x)^2 = 6(3 - 2(-2)) + (2 - 3)^2 = 6(3 + 4) + (-1)^2 = 42 + 1 = 43$

7) Choice E is correct

Use formula of rectangle prism volume. $V = (length)(width)(height) \Rightarrow 2500 = (25)(10)(height) \Rightarrow height = 2500 \div 250 = 10$

8) Choice C is correct

$4 \div \dfrac{1}{3} = 12$

9) Choice B is correct

The diagonal of the square is 4. Let x be the side. Use Pythagorean Theorem: $a^2 + b^2 = c^2$

$x^2 + x^2 = 4^2 \Rightarrow 2x^2 = 4^2 \Rightarrow 2x^2 = 16 \Rightarrow x^2 = 8 \Rightarrow x = \sqrt{8}$

The area of the square is: $\sqrt{8} \times \sqrt{8} = 8$

10) Choice D is correct

Solve for the sum of five numbers.

$$\text{average} = \frac{\text{sum of terms}}{\text{number of terms}} \Rightarrow 26 = \frac{sum\ of\ 5\ numbers}{5} \Rightarrow sum\ of\ 5\ numbers = 26 \times 5 = 130$$

The sum of 5 numbers is 130. If a sixth number 42 is added, then the sum of 6 numbers is

$$130 + 42 = 172.\ average = \frac{\text{sum of terms}}{\text{number of terms}} = \frac{172}{6} = 28.66$$

11) Choice B is correct

ratio of A: $\frac{570}{600} = 0.95$ ratio of B: $\frac{291}{300} = 0.97$ ratio of C: $\frac{665}{700} = 0.95$ ratio of D: $\frac{528}{550} = 0.96$

The maximum ratio is 0.97

12) Choice E is correct

First find percentage of men in city A and percentage of women in city C. Percentage of men in

city A $= \frac{600}{1170}$ and percentage of women in city C $= \frac{665}{1365}$. Find the ratio and simplify. $\frac{\frac{600}{1170}}{\frac{665}{1365}} = \frac{20}{19}$

13) Choice C is correct

$\frac{528 + x}{550} = 1.2 \rightarrow 528 + x = 660 \rightarrow x = 132$

14) Choice E is correct

Jason needs an 70% average to pass for five exams. Therefore, the sum of 5 exams must be at lease $5 \times 70 = 350$.The sum of 4 exams is: $68 + 72 + 85 + 90 = 315$.

The minimum score Jason can earn on his fifth and final test to pass is: $350 - 315 = 35$

15) Choice B is correct

Isolate and solve for $x.\frac{2}{3}x + \frac{1}{6} = \frac{1}{2} \Rightarrow \frac{2}{3}x = \frac{1}{2} - \frac{1}{6} = \frac{1}{3} \Rightarrow \frac{2}{3}x = \frac{1}{3}$ .Multiply both sides by the reciprocal of the coefficient of x. $(\frac{3}{2})\frac{1}{3}x = \frac{1}{3}(\frac{3}{2}) \Rightarrow x = \frac{3}{6} = \frac{1}{2}$

16) Choice B is correct

Use simple interest formula:$I = prt$ (I = interest, p = principal, r = rate, t = time).

$$I = (12,000)(0.045)(2) = 1,080$$

17) Choice D is correct

Simplify. $7x^2y^3(2x^2y)^3 = 7x^2y^3(8x^6y^3) = 56x^8y^6$

18) Choice C is correct

y is the intersection of the three circles. Therefore, it must be even (from circle A), negative (from circle B), and multiple of 6 (from circle C). From the choice, only -6 is even, negative and multiple of 6.

19) Choice C is correct

Three times of 25,000 is 75,000. One sixth of them cancelled their tickets. One sixth of 75,000 equals 12,500 ($\frac{1}{6} \times 75000 = 12500$). 62,500 ($75000 - 12000 = 62500$) fans are attending this week.

20) Choice E is correct

The area of the square is 49 inches. Therefore, the side of the square is square root of the area. $\sqrt{49} = 7$ inches. Four times the side of the square is the perimeter: $4 \times 7 = 28 \ inches$

21) Choice E is correct

$g(x) = -4$, then $f\big(g(x)\big) = f(-4) = 2\,(-4)^3 + 5(-4)^2 + 2(-4) = -128 + 80 - 8 = -56$

22) Choice E is correct

Use the information provided in the question to draw the shape.

Use Pythagorean Theorem: $a^2 + b^2 = c^2$

$50^2 + 120^2 = c^2 \Rightarrow 2,500 + 14,400 = c^2 \Rightarrow 16,900 = c^2 \Rightarrow c = 130$

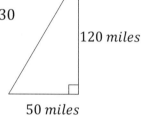

Port A

120 *miles*

50 *miles*

23) Choice B is correct

Plug in 104 for F and then solve for C.

$C = \dfrac{5}{9}\,(F - 32) \Rightarrow C = \dfrac{5}{9}\,(104 - 32) \Rightarrow C = \dfrac{5}{9}\,(72) = 40$

24) Choice A is correct

The width of the rectangle is twice its length. Let x be the length. Then, $width = 2x$

Perimeter of the rectangle is $2\,(width + length) = 2(2x + x) = 72 \Rightarrow 6x = 72 \Rightarrow x = 12$. Length of the rectangle is 12 meters.

25) Choice D is correct

$average = \dfrac{\text{sum of terms}}{\text{number of terms}} \Rightarrow$ (average of 6 numbers) $14 = \dfrac{\text{sum of numbers}}{6} \Rightarrow$ sum of 6 numbers is $14 \times 6 = 84$, (average of 4 numbers) $10 = \dfrac{\text{sum of numbers}}{4} \Rightarrow$ sum of 4 numbers is $10 \times 4 = 40$. $sum\ of\ 6\ numbers - sum\ of\ 4\ numbers = sum\ of\ 2\ numbers$,

$84 - 40 = 44$ average of 2 numbers $= \dfrac{44}{2} = 22$

26) Choice A is correct

First, find the number. Let x be the number. Write the equation and solve for x. 150% of a number is 75, then: $1.5 \times x = 75 \Rightarrow x = 75 \div 1.5 = 50$, 80% of 50 is: $0.8 \times 50 = 40$

27) Choice E is correct

Solve for y. $4x - 2y = 12 \Rightarrow -2y = 12 - 4x \Rightarrow y = 2x - 6$. The slope of the line is 2.

28) Choice B is correct

the population is increased by 10% and 20%. 10% increase changes the population to 110% of original population. For the second increase, multiply the result by 120%.

$(1.10) \times (1.20) = 1.32 = 132\%$. 32 percent of the population is increased after two years.

29) Choice C is correct

The formula for the area of the circle is: $A = \pi r^2$,The area is 36π. Therefore:$A = \pi r^2 \Rightarrow 6\pi = \pi r^2$, Divide both sides by π: $36 = r^2 \Rightarrow r = 6$. Diameter of a circle is $2 \times$ radius. Then:

$Diameter = 2 \times 6 = 12$

30) Choice D is correct

If 20% of a number is 4, what is the number: $20\% \ of \ x = 4 \Rightarrow 0.20 \ x = 4 \Rightarrow x = 4 \div 0.20 = 20$

31) Choice C is correct

Write a proportion and solve for x. $\frac{3}{2} = \frac{x}{26} \Rightarrow 2x = 3 \times 26 \Rightarrow x = 39 \ ft$

32) Choice C is correct

The distance between Jason and Joe is $9 \ miles$. Jason running at $6.5 \ miles \ per \ hour$ and Joe is running at the speed of $8 \ miles \ per \ hour$. Therefore, every hour the distance is $1.5 \ miles$ less.

$9 \div 1.5 = 6$

33) Choice D is correct

The failing rate is 11 out of 44 $= \frac{11}{44}$,Change the fraction to percent:$\frac{11}{44} \times 100\% = 25\%$. 25 percent of students failed. Therefore, 75 percent of students passed the exam.

34) Choice E is correct

$g(x) = -3$, then $f\big(g(x)\big) = f(-3) = 2 \ (-3)^3 + 5(-3)^2 + 2(-3) = -54 + 45 - 6 = -15$

35) Choice E is correct

Let x be the width of the rectangle. Use Pythagorean Theorem:

$a^2 + b^2 = c^2$

$x^2 + 6^2 = 10^2 \Rightarrow x^2 + 36 = 100 \Rightarrow x^2 = 100 - 36 = 64 \Rightarrow x = 8$

Perimeter of the rectangle $= 2 \ (length \ + \ width) = 2 \ (8 \ + \ 6) = 2 \ (14) = 28$

36) Choice B is correct

The perimeter of the trapezoid is 40.herefore, the missing side (height) is

$= 40 - 8 - 12 - 6 = 14$. Area of a trapezoid: $A = \frac{1}{2} h (b_1 + b_2) = \frac{1}{2} (14) (6 + 8) = 98$

37) Choice E is correct

$$f\big(g(x)\big) = 2 \times (\frac{1}{x})^3 + 2 = \frac{2}{x^3} + 2$$

38) Choice D is correct

Use the information provided in the question to draw the shape.

Use Pythagorean Theorem: $a^2 + b^2 = c^2$

$80^2 + 150^2 = c^2 \Rightarrow 6400 + 22500 = c^2 \Rightarrow 28900 = c^2 \Rightarrow c = 170$

39) Choice C is correct

Write the ratio of $5a$ to $2b$. $\frac{5a}{2b} = \frac{1}{10}$. Use cross multiplication and then simplify.

$$5a \times 10 = 2b \times 1 \rightarrow 50a = 2b \rightarrow a = \frac{2b}{50} = \frac{b}{25}$$

Now, find the ratio of a to b. $\frac{a}{b} = \frac{\frac{b}{25}}{b} \rightarrow \frac{b}{25} \div b = \frac{b}{25} \times \frac{1}{b} = \frac{b}{25b} = \frac{1}{25}$

40) Choice A is correct

Plug in the value of x in the equation and solve for y. $2y = \frac{2x^2}{3} + 6 \rightarrow 2y = \frac{2(9)^2}{3} + 6 \rightarrow$

$$2y = \frac{2(81)}{3} + 6 \rightarrow 2y = 54 + 6 = 60 \rightarrow 2y = 60 \rightarrow y = 30$$

41) Choice D is correct

Since $N = 6$, substitute 6 for N in the equation $\frac{x-3}{5} = N$, which gives $\frac{x-3}{5} = 6$. Multiplying both sides of $\frac{x-3}{5} = 6$ by 5 gives $x - 3 = 30$ and then adding 3 to both sides of $x - 3 = 30$ then, $x = 33$.

42) Choice C is correct

$b^{\frac{m}{n}} = \sqrt[n]{b^m}$ For any positive integers m and n. Thus, $b^{\frac{3}{5}} = \sqrt[5]{b^3}$

43) Choice B is correct

The total number of pages read by Sara is 3 (hours she spent reading) multiplied by her rate of reading: $\frac{N pages}{hour} \times 3 hours = 3N$

Similarly, the total number of pages read by Mary is 4 (hours she spent reading) multiplied by her rate of reading: $\frac{M pages}{hour} \times 4 hours = 4M$ the total number of pages read by Sara and Mary is the sum of the total number of pages read by Sara and the total number of pages read by Mary: $3N + 4M$.

44) Choices D and E are correct
First, find the sum of five numbers.

$$\text{average} = \frac{\text{sum of terms}}{\text{number of terms}} \Rightarrow 25 = \frac{\text{sum of 5 numbers}}{5} \Rightarrow \text{sum of 5 numbers} = 25 \times 5 = 125$$

The sum of 5 numbers is 125. If a sixth number that is greater than 42 is added to these numbers, then the sum of 6 numbers must be greater than 162. $125 + 42 = 167$

If the number was 42, then the average of the numbers is:

$$\text{average} = \frac{\text{sum of terms}}{\text{number of terms}} = \frac{167}{6} = 27.83$$

Since the number is bigger than 42. Then, the average of six numbers must be greater than 27.83.

Choices D and E are greater than 27.83.

45) The answer is 28.
Let x be the width of the rectangle. Use Pythagorean Theorem:

$$a^2 + b^2 = c^2$$

$$x^2 + 8^2 = 10^2 \Rightarrow x^2 + 64 = 100 \Rightarrow x^2 = 100 - 64 = 36 \Rightarrow x = 6$$

Perimeter of the rectangle $= 2\,(length + width) = 2\,(8 + 6) = 2\,(14) = 28$

46) Choice D is correct
Solving Systems of Equations by Elimination: Multiply the first equation by (-2), then add it to the second equation.

$$\begin{array}{l} -2(2x + 5y = 11) \\ 4x - 2y = -14 \end{array} \Rightarrow \begin{array}{l} -4x - 10y = -22 \\ 4x - 2y = -14 \end{array} \Rightarrow -12y = -36 \Rightarrow y = 3$$

Plug in the value of y into one of the equations and solve for x.

$$2x + 5(3) = 11 \Rightarrow 2x + 15 = 11 \Rightarrow 2x = -4 \Rightarrow x = -2$$

47) Choice A is correct

Identify the input value. Since the function is in the form $f(x)$ and the question asks to calculate $f(4)$, the input value is four. $f(4) \rightarrow x = 4$, Using the function, input the desired x value. Now substitute 4 in for every x in the function. $f(x) = 3x^2 - 4$, $f(4) = 3(4)^2 - 4$, $f(4) = 48 - 4$, $f(4) = 44$

48) Choice D is correct

Frist factor the function: $f(x) = x^3 + 5x^2 + 6x = x\,(x+2)(x+3)$, To find the zeros, $f(x)$ should be zero. $f(x) = x\,(x+2)(x+3) = 0$, Therefore, the zeros are: $x = 0$, $(x+2) = 0 \Rightarrow x = -2, (x+3) = 0 \Rightarrow x = -3$

49) The answer is: -30

Use PEMDAS (order of operation):

$$5 + 8 \times (-2) - [4 + 22 \times 5] \div 6 = 5 + 8 \times (-2) - [4 + 110] \div 6$$
$$= 5 + 8 \times (-2) - [114] \div 6 = 5 + (-16) - 19 = 5 + (-16) - 19$$
$$= -11 - 19 = -30$$

50) Choice D and E are correct

The equation of a line is in the form of $y = mx + b$, where m is the slope of the line and b is the $y-intercept$ of the line. Two points $(1, 2)$ and $(-1, 6)$ are on line A. Therefore, the slope of the line A is: $slope\ of\ line\ A = \frac{y_2 - y_1}{x_2 - x_1} = \frac{6-2}{-1-1} = \frac{4}{-2} = -2$

The slope of line A is -2. Thus, the formula of the line A is: $y = mx + b = -2x + b$, choose a point and plug in the values of x and y in the equation to solve for b. Let's choose point $(1, 2)$. Then: $y = -2x + b \rightarrow 2 = -2(1) + b \rightarrow b = 2 + 2 = 4$. The equation of line A is: $y = -2x + 4$

Now, let's review the choices provided:

A. $(-1, 2)$ $y = -2x + 4 \rightarrow 2 = -2(-1) + 4 = 6$ This is not true.

B. $(5, 7)$ $y = -2x + 4 \rightarrow 7 = -2(5) + 4 = -6$ This is not true.

C. $(3, 4)$ $y = -2x + 4 \rightarrow 4 = -2(3) + 4 = -2$ This is not true.

D. $(3, -2)$ $y = -2x + 4 \rightarrow -2 = -2(3) + 4 = -2$ This is true!

E. $(6, -8)$ $y = -2x + 4 \rightarrow -8 = -2(6) + 4 = -8$ This is true!

51) Choice C is correct

If $x - a$ is a factor of $g(x)$, then $g(a)$ must equal 0. Based on the table $g(2) = 0$. Therefore, $x - 2$ must be a factor of $g(x)$.

52) Choice C is correct

To solve this problem first solve the equation for c. $\frac{c}{b} = 2$

Multiply by b on both sides. Then: $b \times \frac{c}{b} = 2 \times b \rightarrow c = 2b$.   Now to calculate $\frac{4b}{c}$,

substitute the value for c into the denominator and simplify. $\frac{4b}{c} = \frac{4b}{2b} = \frac{4}{2} = \frac{2}{1} = 2$

53) Choice B is correct

$x + 5 = 8 \rightarrow x = 8 - 5 = 3, 2y - 1 = 5 \rightarrow 2y = 6 \rightarrow y = 3, xy + 15 = 3 \times 3 + 15 = 24$

54) Choice B is correct

The equation $\frac{a-b}{b} = \frac{10}{13}$ can be rewritten as $\frac{a}{b} - \frac{b}{b} = \frac{10}{13}$, from which it follows that $\frac{a}{b} - 1 = \frac{10}{13}$, or $\frac{a}{b} = \frac{10}{13} + 1 = \frac{23}{13}$.

55) Choice A is correct

First write the equation in slope intercept form. Add $2x$ to both sides to get $6y = 2x + 24$. Now divide both sides by 6 to get $y = \frac{1}{3}x + 4$. The slope of this line is $\frac{1}{3}$, so any line that also has a slope of $\frac{1}{3}$ would be parallel to it. Only choice A has a slope of $\frac{1}{3}$.

56) Choice A is correct

Since a box of pen costs \$3, then $3p$ Represents the cost of p boxes of pen. Multiplying this number times 1.085 will increase the cost by the 8.5% for tax. Then add the \$6 shipping fee for the total: $1.085(3p) + 6$

Praxis Core Math Practice Test 3

1) Choice C is correct

Let x be the number. Write the equation and solve for $x.(24 - x) \div x = 3$. Multiply both sides by x. $(24 - x) = 3x$, then add x both sides. $24 = 4x$, now divide both sides by 4.

$x = 6$

2) Choice B is correct

The sum of supplement angles is 180. Let x be that angle. Therefore, $x + 5x = 180$

$6x = 180$, divide both sides by 6: $x = 30$

3) The answer is 90

In the equilateral triangle if x is length of one side of triangle, then the perimeter of the triangle is $3x$. Then $3x = 45 \rightarrow x = 15$ and radius of the circle is: $x = 15$, Then, the perimeter of the circle is: $2\pi r = 2\pi(15) = 30\pi$, $\pi = 3 \rightarrow 30\pi = 30 \times 3 = 90$

4) The answer is 456

$\frac{14}{100}x = 84 \rightarrow x = \frac{84 \times 100}{14} = 600, \frac{1}{8}y = 18 \rightarrow y = 8 \times 18 = 144$

$\rightarrow x - y = 600 - 144 = 456$

5) Choice C is correct

Add the first 5 numbers. $40 + 45 + 50 + 35 + 55 = 225$

To find the distance traveled in the next 5 hours, multiply the average by number of hours.

$Distance = Average \times Rate = 50 \times 5 = 250$, Add both numbers. $250 + 225 = 475$

6) Choice C is correct

Use distance formula: $Distance = Rate \times time \Rightarrow 420 = 50 \times T$, divide both sides by 50. $420 \div 50 = T \Rightarrow T = 8.4\ hours.$Change hours to minutes for the decimal part. $0.4\ hours = 0.4 \times 60 = 24\ minutes.$

7) Choice D is correct

Use Pythagorean Theorem: $a^2 + b^2 = c^2$, $6^2 + 8^2 = c^2 \Rightarrow 100 = c^2 \Rightarrow c = 10$

8) Choice E is correct

Th ratio of boy to girls is $2:3$. Therefore, there are 2 boys out of 5 students. To find the answer, first divide the total number of students by 5, then multiply the result by 2.

$600 \div 5 = 120 \Rightarrow 120 \times 2 = 240$

9) Choice C is correct

Use percent formula:$part = \frac{percent}{100} \times whole$

$$25 = \frac{percent}{100} \times 20 \Rightarrow 25 = \frac{percent \times 20}{100} \Rightarrow 25$$
$$= \frac{percent \times 2}{10}, multiply\ both\ sides\ by\ 10.$$
$250 = percent \times 2$, divide both sides by 2. $\qquad 125 = percent$

10) Choice E is correct

The perimeter of the trapezoid is 54.

Therefore, the missing side (height) is $= 54 - 18 - 12 - 14 = 10$

Area of the trapezoid: $A = \frac{1}{2} h (b_1 + b_2) = \frac{1}{2} (10)(12 + 14) = 130$

11) Choice C is correct

Let x be the number. Write the equation and solve for x. $\frac{2}{3} \times 18 = \frac{2}{5} . x \Rightarrow \frac{2 \times 18}{3} = \frac{2x}{5}$, use cross multiplication to solve for x. $5 \times 36 = 2x \times 3 \Rightarrow 180 = 6x \Rightarrow x = 30$

12) Choice B is correct

To find the discount, multiply the number by $(100\% - rate\ of\ discount)$.

Therefore, for the first discount we get: $(D) (100\% - 20\%) = (D) (0.80) = 0.80\,D$

For increase of 10%: $(0.80\,D)(100\% + 10\%) = (0.80\,D)(1.10) = 0.88\,D = 88\%\ of\ D$

13) Choice B is correct

Use the formula of areas of circles. $Area = \pi r^2 \Rightarrow 25\,\pi = \pi r^2 \Rightarrow 25 = r^2 \Rightarrow r = 5$

Radius of the circle is 5. Now, use the circumference formula: Circumference $= 2\pi r = 2\pi (5) = 10\,\pi$

14) The answer is: -122

Use PEMDAS (order of operation):

$[6 \times (-24) + 8] - (-4) + [4 \times 5] \div 2 = [-144 + 8] - (-4) + [20] \div 2 =$

$[-144 + 8] - (-4) + 10 = [-136] - (-4) + 10 = [-136] + 4 + 10 = -122$

15) Choice C is correct

The question is this: 1.75 is what percent of 1.25? Use percent formula: part $= \frac{percent}{100} \times whole$

$$1.75 = \frac{percent}{100} \times 1.25 \Rightarrow 1.75 = \frac{percent \times 1.25}{100} \Rightarrow 175 = percent \times 1.25$$

$$\Rightarrow percent = \frac{175}{1.25} = 140$$

16) Choice B is correct

Use the information provided in the question to draw the shape.

Use Pythagorean Theorem: $a^2 + b^2 = c^2$

$40^2 + 30^2 = c^2 \Rightarrow 1600 + 900 = c^2 \Rightarrow 2500 = c^2 \Rightarrow c = 50$

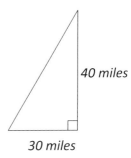

40 miles

30 miles

17) Choice B is correct

The question is this: 530.40 is what percent of 624?

Use percent formula: part $= \frac{percent}{100} \times whole$. $530.40 = \frac{percent}{100} \times 624 \Rightarrow$

$530.40 = \frac{percent \times 624}{100} \Rightarrow 53040 = percent \times 624 \Rightarrow percent = \frac{530.40}{624} = 85$

530.40 is 85% of 624. Therefore, the discount is: $100\% - 85\% = 15\%$

18) Choice B is correct

If the score of Mia was 60, therefore the score of Ava is 30. Since, the score of Emma was half as that of Ava, therefore, the score of Emma is 15.

19) Choice B is correct

Let x be the smallest number. Then, these are the numbers: $x, x + 1, x + 2, x + 3, x + 4$

$average = \frac{\text{sum of terms}}{\text{number of terms}} \Rightarrow 38 = \frac{x+(x+1)+(x+2)+(x+3)+(x+4)}{5} \Rightarrow 38 = \frac{5x+10}{5} \Rightarrow 190 = 5x + 10 \Rightarrow 180 = 5x \Rightarrow x = 36$

20) Choice C is correct

The area of the floor is: $6\ cm \times 24\ cm = 144\ cm^2$, The number is tiles needed $=$

$$144 \div 8 = 18$$

21) Choice C is correct

The weight of 12.2 meters of this rope is: $12.2 \times 600\ g = 7320\ g$,

$1\ kg = 1000\ g$, therefore, $7320\ g \div 1000 = 7.32\ kg$

22) Choice C is correct

4% of the volume of the solution is alcohol. Let x be the volume of the solution.

Then: $4\%\ of\ x = 24\ ml \Rightarrow 0.04\ x = 24 \Rightarrow x = 24 \div 0.04 = 600$

23) Choice B is correct

$average = \frac{\text{sum of terms}}{\text{number of terms}}$, The sum of the weight of all girls is: $18 \times 60 = 1080\ kg$, The sum of the weight of all boys is: $32 \times 62 = 1984\ kg$, The sum of the weight of all students is: $1080 + 1984 = 3064\ kg$, average $= \frac{3064}{50} = 61.28$

24) Choice C is correct

Let x be the original price. If the price of a laptop is decreased by 10% to \$360, then: $90\%\ of\ x = 360 \Rightarrow 0.90x = 360 \Rightarrow x = 360 \div 0.90 = 400$

25) Choice E is correct

Surface Area of a cylinder $= 2\pi r\ (r + h)$, The radius of the cylinder is 8 inches and its height is 12 inches. Surface Area of a cylinder $= 2\ (\pi)\ (8)\ (8 + 12) = 320\ \pi$

26) Choice E is correct

$average = \frac{\text{sum of terms}}{\text{number of terms}} \Rightarrow 18 = \frac{13+15+20+x}{4} \Rightarrow 72 = 48 + x \Rightarrow x = 24$

27) Choice C is correct

Let x be the original price. If the price of the sofa is decreased by 25% to \$420, then: $75\%\ of\ x = 420 \Rightarrow 0.75x = 420 \Rightarrow x = 420 \div 0.75 = 560$

28) Choice C is correct

Use simple interest formula: $I = prt$, ($I = $ interest, $p = $ principal, $r = $ rate, $t = $ time)

$I = (8,000)(0.045)(5) = 1,800$

29) Choice E is correct

$(4.2 \times 10^6) \times (2.6 \times 10^{-5}) = (4.2 \times 2.6) \times (10^6 \times 10^{-5}) = 10.92 \times (10^{6 + (-5)})$
$= 1.092 \times 10^2$

30) Choice E is correct

The formula of the volume of pyramid is: $V = \frac{l \times w \times h}{3}$. The length and width of the pyramid is $6\ cm$ and its height is $12\ cm$. Therefore: $V = \frac{6 \times 6 \times 12}{3} = 144\ cm^3$

31) Choice E is correct

Simplify: $4(x + 1) = 6(x - 4) + 20, 4x + 4 = 6x - 24 + 20, 4x + 4 = 6x - 4$

Subtract $4x$ from both sides: $4 = 2x - 4$, Add 4 to both sides: $8 = 2x, 4 = x$

32) Choice E is correct

Use distributive property: $2x(4 + 2y) = 8x + 4xy = 4xy + 8x$

33) Choice E is correct

$y = 4ab + 3b^3$, plug in the values of a and b in the equation: $a = 2$ and $b = 3$,

$y = 4(2)(3) + 3(3)^3 = 24 + 3(27) = 24 + 81 = 105$

34) Choices A and B are correct

(If you selected 3 choices and 2 of them are correct, then you get one point. If you answered 2 or 3 choices and one of them is correct, you receive one point. If you selected more than 3 choices, you won't get any point for this question.)

Volume of the cube is less than $64\ m^3$. Use the formula of volume of cubes.

$volume = (one\ side)^3 \Rightarrow 64 > \Rightarrow 64 > (one\ side)^3$. Find the cube root of both sides. Then: $4 > one\ side$. The side of the cube is less than 4. Only choices A and B are less than 4.

35) The answer is 3 or 6

The x-intercepts of the quadratic equation represented by $y = x^2 - 9x + 18$ in the xy-plane are the values of x for which y is equal to 0. The factored form of the equation, $y = (x - 3)(x - 6)$, shows that y equals 0 if and only if $x = 3$ or $x = 6$. Thus, the x-intercepts of the quadratic are 3 and 6.

36) Choice C is correct

Set of number that are not composite between 1 and 25: A= {1, 2, 3, 5, 7, 11, 13, 17, 19, 23}

$$\text{Probability} = \frac{number\ of\ desired\ outcomes}{number\ of\ total\ outcomes} = \frac{10}{25} = \frac{2}{5}$$

37) Choice B is correct

Plug in each pair of number in the equation:

A. $(2, 1)$: $2(2) + 4(1) = 8$
B. $(-1, 3)$: $2(-1) + 4(3) = 10$
C. $(-2, 2)$: $2(-2) + 4(2) = 4$
D. $(2, 2)$: $2(2) + 4(2) = 12$
E. $(2, 8)$: $2(2) + 4(8) = 36$

Only Choice B is correct.

38) Choice B is correct

Use this formula: Percent of Change: $\dfrac{New\ Value - Old\ Value}{Old\ Value} \times 100\%$

$\dfrac{16000 - 20000}{20000} \times 100\% = -20\%$ and $\dfrac{12800 - 16000}{16000} \times 100\% = -20\%$

39) Choice D is correct

The relationship among all sides of special right triangle

$30° - 60° - 90°$ is provided in this triangle:

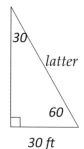

In this triangle, the opposite side of $30°$ angle is half of the hypotenuse.

Draw the shape of this question:

The latter is the hypotenuse. Therefore, the latter is $60\ ft$

40) Choices D and E are correct

(If you selected 3 choices and 2 of them are correct, then you get one point. If you answered 2 or 3 choices and one of them is correct, you receive one point. If you selected more than 3 choices, you won't get any point for this question.)

Area of the circle is less than $81\pi\ ft^2$. Use the formula of areas of circles.

$Area = \pi r^2 \Rightarrow 81\pi > \pi r^2 \Rightarrow 81 > r^2 \Rightarrow r < 9$

Radius of the circle is less than $9\ ft$. Therefore, the diameter of the circle is less than $18\ ft$. Only choices D and E are less than $18 ft$.

41) Choice C is correct

Method 1: Plugin the values of x and y provided in the options into both equations.

A. $(4,3)$ $x + y = 0 \to 4 + 3 \neq 0$

B. $(5,4)$ $x + y = 0 \to 5 + 4 \neq 0$

C. $(4,-4)$ $x + y = 0 \to 4 + (-4) = 0$

D. $(4,-6)$ $x + y = 0 \to 4 + (-6) \neq 0$

E. $(2,-6)$ $x + y = 0 \to 2 + (-6) \neq 0$

Only option C is correct.

Method 2: Multiplying each side of $x + y = 0$ by 2 gives $2x + 2y = 0$. Then, adding the corresponding side of $2x + 2y = 0$ and $4x - 2y = 24$ gives $6x = 24$. Dividing each side of $6x = 24$ by 6 gives $x = 4$. Finally, substituting 4 for x in $x + y = 0$, or $y = -4$. Therefore, the solution to the given system of equations is $(4, -4)$.

42) Choice A is correct

If $f(x) = 3x + 4(x + 1) + 2$, then find $f(3x)$ by substituting $3x$ for every x in the function. This gives: $f(3x) = 3(3x) + 4(3x + 1) + 2$

It simplifies to: $f(3x) = 3(3x) + 4(3x + 1) + 2 = 9x + 12x + 4 + 2 = 21x + 6$

43) Choice C is correct

First, find the equation of the line. All lines through the origin are of the form $y = mx$, so the equation is $y = \frac{2}{3}x$. Of the given choices, only choice C (9,6), satisfies this equation:

$$y = \frac{2}{3}x \to 6 = \frac{2}{3}(9) = 6$$

44) Choice C is correct

$(3n^2 + 4n + 6) - (2n^2 - 5)$.   Add like terms together: $3n^2 - 2n^2 = n^2$

$4n$ doesn't have like terms. $6 - (-5) = 11$

Combine these terms into one expression to find the answer: $n^2 + 4n + 11$

45) Choice C is correct

You can find the possible values of a and b in $(ax + 4)(bx + 3)$ by using the given equation $a + b = 7$ and finding another equation that relates the variables a and b. Since $(ax + 4)(bx + 3) = 10x^2 + cx + 12$, expand the left side of the equation to obtain

$abx^2 + 4bx + 3ax + 12 = 10x^2 + cx + 12$

Since ab is the coefficient of x^2 on the left side of the equation and 10 is the coefficient of x^2 on the right side of the equation, it must be true that $ab = 10$

The coefficient of x on the left side is $4b + 3a$ and the coefficient of x in the right side is c. Then: $4b + 3a = c$, $a + b = 7$, then: $a = 7 - b$

Now, plug in the value of a in the equation $ab = 10$. Then:

$ab = 10 \rightarrow (7-b)b = 10 \rightarrow 7b - b^2 = 10$

Add $-7b + b^2$ both sides. Then: $b^2 - 7b + 10 = 0$

Solve for b using the factoring method. $b^2 - 7b + 10 = 0 \rightarrow (b-5)(b-2) = 0$

Thus, either $b = 2$ and $a = 5$, or $b = 5$ and $a = 2$. If $b = 2$ and $a = 5$, then

$4b + 3a = c \rightarrow 4(2) + 3(5) = c \rightarrow c = 23$. If $5 = 2$ and $a = 2$, then, $4b + 3a = c \rightarrow 4(5) + 3(2) = c \rightarrow c = 26$. Therefore, the two possible values for c are 23 and 26.

46) Choice A is correct

To rewrite $\dfrac{1}{\frac{1}{x-6}+\frac{1}{x+4}}$, first simplify $\dfrac{1}{x-6} + \dfrac{1}{x+4}$.

$\dfrac{1}{x-6} + \dfrac{1}{x+4} = \dfrac{1(x+4)}{(x-6)(x+4)} + \dfrac{1(x-5)}{(x+4)(x-6)} = \dfrac{(x+4)+(x-6)}{(x+4)(x-6)}$

Then: $\dfrac{1}{\frac{1}{x-6}+\frac{1}{x+4}} = \dfrac{1}{\frac{(x+4)+(x-6)}{(x+4)(x-6)}} = \dfrac{(x-6)(x+4)}{(x-6)+(x+4)}$. (Remember, $\dfrac{1}{\frac{1}{x}} = x$)

This result is equivalent to the expression in choice A.

47) Choice B is correct

Since $(0,0)$ is a solution to the system of inequalities, substituting 0 for x and 0 for y in the given system must result in two true inequalities. After this substitution, $y < a - x$ becomes $0 < a$, and $y > x + b$ becomes $0 > b$. Hence, a is positive and b is negative. Therefore, $a > b$.

48) Choice D is correct

First find the slope of the line using the slope formula. $m = \dfrac{y_2 - y_1}{x_2 - x_1}$

Substituting in the known information. $(x_1, y_1) = (2, 4), \quad (x_2, y_2) = (4, 5)$

$m = \dfrac{5-4}{4-2} = \dfrac{1}{2}$

Now the slope to find the equation of the line passing through these points. $y = mx + b$

Choose one of the points and plug in the values of x and y in the equation to solve for b.

Let's choose point $(4, 5)$. Then: $y = mx + b \rightarrow 5 = \frac{1}{2}(4) + b \rightarrow 5 = 2 + b \rightarrow b = 5 - 2 = 3$

The equation of the line is: $y = \frac{1}{2}x + 3$

Now, plug in the points provided in the choices into the equation of the line.

A. $(9, 9)$ $y = \frac{1}{2}x + 3 \rightarrow 9 = \frac{1}{2}(9) + 3 \rightarrow 9 = 7.5$ This is NOT true.

B. $(9, 6)$ $y = \frac{1}{2}x + 3 \rightarrow 6 = \frac{1}{2}(9) + 3 \rightarrow 6 = 7.5$ This is NOT true.

C. $(6, 9)$ $y = \frac{1}{2}x + 3 \rightarrow 9 = \frac{1}{2}(6) + 3 \rightarrow 9 = 6$ This is NOT true.

D. $(6, 6)$ $y = \frac{1}{2}x + 3 \rightarrow 6 = \frac{1}{2}(6) + 3 \rightarrow 6 = 6$ This is true!

E. $(0, 9)$ $y = \frac{1}{2}x + 3 \rightarrow 9 = \frac{1}{2}(0) + 3 \rightarrow 9 = 3$ This is NOT true.

Therefore, the only point from the choices that lies on the line is $(6, 6)$.

49) Choice B is correct

The input value is 4. Then: $x = 4$

$f(x) = x^2 - 3x \rightarrow f(4) = 4^2 - 3(4) = 16 - 12 = 4$

50) Choice B is correct

To solve this problem, first recall the equation of a line: $y = mx + b$

Where $m = slope.$ $y = y - intercept$

Remember that slope is the rate of change that occurs in a function and that the $y -$intercept is the y value corresponding to $x = 0$. Since the height of John's plant is 6 inches tall when he gets it. Time (or x) is zero. The plant grows 4 inches per year. Therefore, the rate of change of the plant's height is 4. The $y -$intercept represents the starting height of the plant which is 6 inches.

51) Choice C is correct

Multiplying each side of $\frac{3}{x} = \frac{12}{x-9}$ by $x(x-9)$ gives $3(x-9) = 12(x)$, distributing the 3 over the values within the parentheses yields $x - 9 = 4x$ or $x = -3$.

Therefore, the value of $\frac{x}{6} = \frac{-3}{6} = -\frac{1}{2}$.

52) Choice C is correct

In order to figure out what the equation of the graph is, fist find the vertex. From the graph we can determine that the vertex is at $(1,2)$. We can use vertex form to solve for the equation of this graph. Recall vertex form, $y = a(x - h)^2 + k$, where h is the x coordinate of the vertex, and k is the y coordinate of the vertex. Plugging in our values, you get $= a(x - 1)^2 + 2$, To solve for a, we need to pick a point on the graph and plug it into the equation. Let's pick $(-1, 10)$, $10 = a(-1 - 1)^2 + 2$

$10 = a(-2)^2 + 2,$ $\qquad\qquad 10 = 4a + 2,$ $\qquad 8 = 4a,$ $\qquad a = 2$

Now the equation is: $y = 2(x - 1)^2 + 2$

Let's expand this, $y = 2(x^2 - 2x + 1) + 2$, $y = 2x^2 - 4x + 2 + 2$

$y = 2x^2 - 4x + 4.$ $\qquad$ The equation in Choice C is the same.

53) Choice C is correct

The line passes through the origin, $(6, m)$ and $(m, 12)$. Any two of these points can be used to find the slope of the line. Since the line passes through $(0, 0)$ and $(6, m)$, the slope of the line is equal to $\frac{m-0}{6-0} = \frac{m}{6}$. Similarly, since the line passes through $(0, 0)$ and $(m, 12)$, the slope of the line is equal to $\frac{12-0}{m-0} = \frac{12}{m}$. Since each expression gives the slope of the same line, it must be true that $\frac{m}{6} = \frac{12}{m}$, Using cross multiplication gives

$\frac{m}{6} = \frac{12}{m} \rightarrow m^2 = 72 \rightarrow m = \pm\sqrt{72} = \pm\sqrt{36 \times 2} = \pm\sqrt{36} \times \sqrt{2} = \pm6\sqrt{2}$

54) Choice B is correct

It is given that $g(6) = 4$. Therefore, to find the value of $f(g(6))$, then $f(g(6)) = f(4) = 7$

55) Choice A is correct

Area of the triangle is: $\frac{1}{2} AD \times BC$ and AD is perpendicular to BC. Triangle ADC is a $30° - 60° - 90°$ right triangle. The relationship among all sides of right triangle $30° - 60° - 90°$ is provided in the following triangle: In this triangle, the opposite side of $30°$ angle is half of the hypotenuse. And the opposite side of $60°$ is opposite of $30° \times \sqrt{3}$

$CD = 4$, then $AD = 4 \times \sqrt{3}$

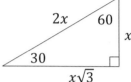

Area of the triangle ABC is: $\frac{1}{2} AD \times BC = \frac{1}{2} 4\sqrt{3} \times 8 = 16\sqrt{3}$

56) Choice B is correct

A linear equation is a relationship between two variables, x and y, and can be written in the form of $y = mx + b$. A non-proportional linear relationship takes on the form $y = mx + b$, where $b \neq 0$ and its graph is a line that does not cross through the origin. Only in graph B, the line does not pass through the origin

Praxis Core Math Practice Test 4

1) Choice E is correct

$g(x) = -2$, then $f(g(x)) = f(-2) = 3(-2)^3 + 5(-2)^2 + 2(-2) = -24 + 20 - 4 = -8$

2) Choice E is correct

Let x be the width of the rectangle. Use Pythagorean Theorem:

$a^2 + b^2 = c^2$

$x^2 + 8^2 = 10^2 \Rightarrow x^2 + 64 = 100 \Rightarrow x^2 = 100 - 64 = 36 \Rightarrow x = 6$

Perimeter of the rectangle = $2 \, (length \, + \, width) = 2 \, (8 + 6) = 2 \, (14) = 28$

3) Choice E is correct

$x = \frac{1}{3}$ and $y = \frac{9}{21}$, substitute the values of x and y in the expression and simplify:

$\frac{1}{x} \div \frac{y}{3} \rightarrow \frac{1}{\frac{1}{3}} \div \frac{\frac{9}{21}}{3} \rightarrow \frac{1}{\frac{1}{3}} = 3$ and $\frac{\frac{9}{21}}{3} = \frac{9}{63} = \frac{1}{7}$. Then: $\frac{1}{\frac{1}{3}} \div \frac{\frac{9}{21}}{3} = 3 \div \frac{1}{7} = 3 \times 7 = 21$

4) Choice A is correct

$$average\ (mean) = \frac{sum\ of\ terms}{number\ of\ terms} \Rightarrow 85 = \frac{sum\ of\ terms}{50} \Rightarrow sum = 85 \times 50 = 4250$$

The difference of 94 and 69 is 25. Therefore, 25 should be subtracted from the sum.

$$4250 - 25 = 4225, mean = \frac{sum\ of\ terms}{number\ of\ terms} \Rightarrow mean = \frac{4225}{50} = 84.5$$

5) Choice D is correct

Solve for x. $x - 4 \le 4x - 8 < 16 \Rightarrow$ (add 8 all sides) $-4 + 8 < 4x - 8 + 8 < 16 + 8 \Rightarrow$

$4 < 4x < 24 \Rightarrow$ (divide all sides by 4) $1 \le x < 6$. x is between 1 and 6. Choice D represents this inequality.

6) Choice E is correct

Use formula of rectangle prism volume.

$$V = (length)\ (width)\ (height) \Rightarrow 2000 = (25)\ (10)\ (height) \Rightarrow height$$
$$= 2000 \div 250 = 8$$

7) Choice C is correct

To find the number of possible outfit combinations, multiply number of options for each factor:

$3 \times 7 \times 4 = 84$

8) Choice B is correct

The diagonal of the square is 8. Let x be the side. Use Pythagorean Theorem: $a^2 + b^2 = c^2$

$x^2 + x^2 = 8^2 \Rightarrow 2x^2 = 8^2 \Rightarrow 2x^2 = 64 \Rightarrow x^2 = 32 \Rightarrow x = \sqrt{32}$

The area of the square is: $\sqrt{32} \times \sqrt{32} = 32$

9) Choice A is correct

The width of the rectangle is twice its length. Let x be the length. Then, $width = 2x$

Perimeter of the rectangle is $2\ (width + length) = 2(2x + x) = 60 \Rightarrow 6x = 60 \Rightarrow x = 10$

Length of the rectangle is 10 meters.

10) Choice D is correct

$average = \frac{sum\ of\ terms}{number\ of\ terms} \Rightarrow$ (average of 6 numbers) $12 = \frac{sum\ of\ numbers}{6} \Rightarrow$ sum of 6 numbers is $12 \times 6 = 72$,

(average of 4 numbers) $10 = \frac{sum\ of\ numbers}{4} \Rightarrow$ sum of 4 numbers is $10 \times 4 = 40$

sum of 6 numbers − sum of 4 numbers = sum of 2 numbers

$72 - 40 = 32$, average of 2 numbers $= \frac{32}{2} = 16$

11) Choice C is correct

Solve for the sum of five numbers.

$average = \frac{sum\ of\ terms}{number\ of\ terms} \Rightarrow 24 = \frac{sum\ of\ 5\ numbers}{5} \Rightarrow$ sum of 5 numbers $= 24 \times 5 = 120$

The sum of 5 numbers is 120. If a sixth number 42 is added, then the sum of 6 numbers is

$120 + 42 = 162$, $average = \frac{sum\ of\ terms}{number\ of\ terms} = \frac{162}{6} = 27$

12) Choice D is correct

Th ratio of boy to girls is $4:7$. Therefore, there are 4 boys out of 11 students. To find the answer, first divide the total number of students by 11, then multiply the result by 4.

$66 \div 11 = 6 \Rightarrow 6 \times 4 = 24$, There are 24 boys and 42 $(66 - 24)$ girls. So, 18 more boys should be enrolled to make the ratio $1:1$.

13) Choice D is correct

Jason needs an 76% average to pass for five exams. Therefore, the sum of 5 exams must be at lease $5 \times 76 = 380$, The sum of 4 exams is: $68 + 72 + 85 + 90 = 315$.

The minimum score Jason can earn on his fifth and final test to pass is: $380 - 315 = 65$

14) Choice A is correct
Let x be the integer. Then: $2x - 5 = 53$. Add 5 both sides: $2x = 58$, Divide both sides by 2:

$x = 29$

15) Choice B is correct

Use simple interest formula: $I = prt$, (I = interest, p = principal, r = rate, t = time)

$I = (12000)(0.035)(2) = 840$

16) Choice D is correct

Simplify. $6x^2y^3(2x^2y)^3 = 6x^2y^3(8x^6y^3) = 48x^8y^6$

17) Choice C is correct

Surface Area of a cylinder $= 2\pi r(r + h)$, The radius of the cylinder is 6 inches and its height is 12 inches. π is about 3.14. Then: Surface Area of a cylinder $= 2(\pi)(6)(6 + 12) = 216\,\pi = 678.24$

18) Choice E is correct

Use Pythagorean Theorem: $a^2 + b^2 = c^2$

$80^2 + 150^2 = c^2 \Rightarrow 6400 + 22500 = c^2 \Rightarrow 28900 = c^2 \Rightarrow c = 170$

19) Choice E is correct

Plug in 104 for F and then solve for C.

$C = \dfrac{5}{9}(F - 32) \Rightarrow C = \dfrac{5}{9}(140 - 32) \Rightarrow C = \dfrac{5}{9}(108) = 60$

20) Choice A is correct

First, find the number. Let x be the number. Write the equation and solve for x.

150% of a number is 75, then: $1.5 \times x = 75 \Rightarrow x = 75 \div 1.5 = 50$

95% of 50 is: $0.95 \times 50 = 47.5$

21) Choice C is correct

the population is increased by 15% and 20%. 15% increase changes the population to 115% of original population. For the second increase, multiply the result by 120%.

$(1.15) \times (1.20) = 1.38 = 138\%$. 38 percent of the population is increased after two years.

22) Choice C is correct

Three times of 24,000 is 72,000. One sixth of them cancelled their tickets. One sixth of 72,000 equals 12,000 $(\frac{1}{6} \times 72000 = 12000)$. 60,000 $(72000 - 12000 = 60000)$ fans are attending this week.

23) Choice E is correct

The area of the square is 64 inches. Therefore, the side of the square is square root of the area. $\sqrt{64} = 8$ inches. Four times the side of the square is the perimeter: $4 \times 8 = 32 \ inches$

24) Choice D is correct

The equation of a line is in the form of $y = mx + b$, where m is the slope of the line and b is the $y - intercept$ of the line. Two points $(4,3)$ and $(3,2)$ are on line A. Therefore, the slope of the line A is: $slope \ of \ line \ A = \dfrac{y_2 - y_1}{x_2 - x_1} = \dfrac{2-3}{3-4} = \dfrac{-1}{-1} = 1$. The slope of line A is 1. Thus, the formula of the line A is: $y = mx + b = x + b$, choose a point and plug in the values of x and y in the equation to solve for b. Let's choose point $(4, 3)$. Then: $y = x + b \to 3 = 4 + b \to b = 3 - 4 = -1$

The equation of line A is: $y = x - 1$. Now, let's review the choices provided:

A. $(-1, 2)$ $y = x - 1 \to 2 = -1 - 1 = -2$ This is not true.

B. $(5, 7)$ $y = x - 1 \to 7 = 5 - 1 = 4$ This is not true.

C. $(3, 4)$ $\quad\quad\quad\quad\quad\quad$ $y = x - 1 \rightarrow 4 = 3 - 1 = 2$ $\quad\quad$ This is not true.

D. $(-1, -2)$ $\quad\quad\quad\quad\quad$ $y = x - 1 \rightarrow -2 = -1 - 1 = -2$ $\quad$ This is true!

E. $(-7, -9)$ $\quad\quad\quad\quad\quad$ $y = x - 1 \rightarrow -9 = -7 - 1 = -8$ $\quad$ This is not true!

25) Choice E is correct

$g(x) = -2$, then $f(g(x)) = f(-2) = 2(-2)^3 + 5(-2)^2 + 2(-2) = -16 + 20 - 4 = 0$

26) Choice E is correct

The formula for the area of the circle is: $A = \pi r^2$ .The area is 64π. Therefore:$A = \pi r^2 \Rightarrow 64\pi = \pi r^2$

Divide both sides by π:$64 = r^2 \Rightarrow r = 8$. Diameter of a circle is $2 \times$ radius. Then:

Diameter $= 2 \times 8 = 16$

27) Choice C is correct

Write a proportion and solve for $x.\frac{3}{2} = \frac{x}{22} \Rightarrow 2x = 3 \times 22 \Rightarrow x = 33 \, ft$

28) Choice A is correct

Use FOIL method. $(4x + 2y)(2x - y) = 8x^2 - 4xy + 4xy - 2y^2 = 8x^2 - 2y^2$

29) Choice D is correct

To solve absolute values equations, write two equations. $x - 10$ could be positive 3, or negative 3. Therefore, $x - 10 = 3 \Rightarrow x = 13$,$x - 10 = -3 \Rightarrow x = 7$, Find the product of solutions:

$$7 \times 13 = 91$$

30) Choice B is correct

The equation of a line in slope intercept form is: $y = mx + b$. Solve for y. $4x - 2y = 8 \Rightarrow -2y = 8 - 4x \Rightarrow y = (8 - 4x) \div (-2) \Rightarrow y = 2x - 4$. The slope is 2. The slope of the line perpendicular to this line is: $m_1 \times m_2 = -1 \Rightarrow 2 \times m_2 = -1 \Rightarrow m_2 = -\frac{1}{2}$

31) Choice C is correct

Plug in the value of x and y. $x = 3$ and $y = -2$,

$5(x - 2y) + (2 - x)^2 = 5(3 - 2(-2)) + (2 - 3)^2 = 5(3 + 4) + (-1)^2 = 35 + 1 = 36$

32) Choice E is correct

The distance between Jason and Joe is 15 miles. Jason running at 5.5 miles per hour and Joe is running at the speed of 7 miles per hour. Therefore, every hour the distance is 1.5 miles less.

$15 \div 1.5 = 10$

33) Choice D is correct

The failing rate is 11 out of 88 $= \frac{11}{88}$, Change the fraction to percent: $\frac{11}{88} \times 100\% = 12.5\%$

12.5 percent of students failed. Therefore, 87.5 percent of students passed the exam.

34) The answer is 7.

Solving Systems of Equations by Elimination

$$3x - 4y = -16$$
$$-x + 2y = 10$$
Multiply the second equation by 3, then add it to the first equation.

$$\frac{3x - 4y = -16}{3(-x + 2y = 10)} \Rightarrow \frac{3x - 4y = -16}{-3x + 6y = 30)} \Rightarrow 2y = 14 \Rightarrow y = 7$$

35) Choice B is correct

The area of trapezoid is: $\left(\frac{8+12}{2}\right) \times x = 100 \rightarrow 10x = 100 \rightarrow x = 10. \ y = \sqrt{3^2 + 4^2} = 5$

Perimeter is: $12 + 10 + 8 + 5 = 35$

36) Choice C is correct

Set of number that are not composite between 1 and 25: $A = \{1, 2, 3, 5, 7, 11, 13, 17, 19, 23\}$

$$\text{Probability} = \frac{number\ of\ desired\ outcomes}{number\ of\ total\ outcomes} = \frac{10}{25} = \frac{2}{5}$$

37) Choice D is correct

Check each choice provided:

A. 1 $\frac{4+5+8+11+12}{5} = \frac{40}{5} = 8$

B. 4 $\frac{1+5+8+11+12}{5} = \frac{37}{5} = 7.4$

C. 5 $\frac{1+4+8+11+12}{5} = \frac{36}{5} = 7.2$

D. 11 $\frac{1+4+5+8+12}{5} = \frac{30}{5} = 6$

E. 12 $\frac{1+4+5+8+11}{5} = \frac{29}{5} = 5.8$

38) The answer is 260.

The perimeter of the trapezoid is 64.

Therefore, the missing side (height) is $= 64 - 18 - 12 - 14 = 20$

Area of a trapezoid: $A = \frac{1}{2} h (b_1 + b_2) = \frac{1}{2} (20) (12 + 14) = 260$

39) Choice C is correct

Plug in the value of each choice in the inequality.

A. $1 (1 - 2)^2 + 1 > 3(1) - 1 \rightarrow 2 > 2$ No!

B. $6 (6 - 2)^2 + 1 > 3(6) - 1 \rightarrow 17 > 17$ No!

C. $8 (8 - 2)^2 + 1 > 3(8) - 1 \rightarrow 37 > 23$ Bingo!

D. $3 (3 - 2)^2 + 1 > 3(3) - 1 \rightarrow 2 > 8$ No!

E. $4 (4 - 2)^2 + 1 > 3(4) - 1 \rightarrow 5 > 11$ No!

40) The answer is 3.

Let x be the length of an edge of cube, then the volume of a cube is: $V = x^3$

The surface area of cube is: $SA = 6x^2$, The volume of cube A is $\frac{1}{2}$ of its surface area. Then: $x^3 = \frac{6x^2}{2} \rightarrow x^3 = 3x^2$, divide both side of the equation by x^2. Then: $\frac{x^3}{x^2} = \frac{3x^2}{x^2} \rightarrow x = 3$

41) Choice D is correct

Since $N = 7$, substitute 7 for N in the equation $\frac{x-3}{5} = N$, which gives $\frac{x-3}{5} = 7$. Multiplying both sides of $\frac{x-3}{5} = 7$ by 5 gives $x - 3 = 35$ and then adding 3 to both sides of $x - 3 = 35$ then, $x = 38$.

42) Choice C is correct

$b^{\frac{m}{n}} = \sqrt[n]{b^m}$ For any positive integers m and n. Thus, $b^{\frac{4}{5}} = \sqrt[5]{b^4}$.

43) Choice C is correct

First find the value of b, and then find $f(4)$. Since $f(2) = 35$, substuting 2 for x and 35 for $f(x)$ gives $35 = b(2)^2 + 15 = 4b + 15$. Solving this equation gives $b = 5$. Thus

$$f(x) = 5x^2 + 15, \quad f(4) = 5(4)^2 + 15 \rightarrow f(4) = 80 + 15, \quad f(4) = 95$$

44) Choice D is correct

Multiplying each side of $-3x - y = 6$ by 2 gives $-6x - 2y = 12$. Adding each side of $-6x - 2y = 12$ to the corresponding side of $6x + 4y = 10$ gives $2y = 22$ or $y = 11$. Finally, substituting 11 for y in $6x + 4y = 10$ gives $6x + 4(11) = 10$ or $x = -\frac{17}{3}$.

45) Choice A is correct

Identify the input value. Since the function is in the form $f(x)$ and the question asks to calculate $f(3)$, the input value is four. $f(3) \rightarrow x = 3$ Using the function, input the desired x value.

Now substitute 4 in for every x in the function. $f(x) = 3x^2 - 4$, $f(3) = 3(3)^2 - 4$, $f(3) = 27 - 4$, $f(3) = 23$

46) Choice D is correct

The problem asks for the sum of the roots of the quadratic equation $2n^2 + 16n + 24 = 0$. Dividing each side of the equation by 2 gives $n^2 + 8n + 12 = 0$. If the roots of

$n^2 + 8n + 12 = 0$ are n_1 and n_2, then the equation can be factored as

$n^2 + 8n + 12 = (n - n_1)(n - n_2) = 0$. Looking at the coefficient of n on each side of

$n^2 + 8n + 12 = (n + 6)(n + 2)$ gives $n = -6$ or $n = -2$, then, $-6 + (-2) = -8$

47) Choice D is correct

The x-intercepts of the parabola represented by $y = x^2 - 8x + 12$ in the xy-plane are the values of x for which y is equal to 0. The factored form of the equation, $y = (x - 2)(x - 6)$, shows that y equals 0 if and only if $x = 2$ or $x = 6$. Thus, the factored form $y = (x - 2)(x - 6)$, displays the x-intercepts of the parabola as the constants 2 and 6.

48) Choice C is correct

If $x - a$ is a factor of $g(x)$, then $g(a)$ must equal 0. Based on the table $g(1) = 0$. Therefore, $x - 1$ must be a factor of $g(x)$.

49) Choice C is correct

To solve this problem first solve the equation for c. $\frac{c}{b} = 2$

Multiply by b on both sides. Then: $b \times \frac{c}{b} = 2 \times b \rightarrow c = 2b$. Now to calculate $\frac{6b}{c}$, substitute the value for c into the denominator and simplify. $\frac{6b}{c} = \frac{6b}{2b} = \frac{6}{2} = 3$

50) Choice B is correct

Simplify the numerator: $\frac{x + (5x)^2 + (3x)^3}{x} = \frac{x + 5^2 x^2 + 3^3 x^3}{x} = \frac{x + 25x^2 + 27x^3}{x}$

Pull an x out of each term in the numerator. $\frac{x(1 + 25x + 27x^2)}{x}$

The x in the numerator and the x in the denominator cancel:

$1 + 25x + 27x^2 = 27x^2 + 25x + 1$

51) The answer is 120
To find the number of possible outfit combinations, multiply number of options for each factor:

$6 \times 4 \times 5 = 120$

52) The answer is 200
Th ratio of boy to girls is $2:3$. Therefore, there are 2 boys out of 5 students. To find the answer, first divide the total number of students by 5, then multiply the result by 2.

$500 \div 5 = 100 \Rightarrow 100 \times 2 = 200$

53) Choice A is correct

$x - 2 \geq 3 \to x \geq 3 + 2 \to x \geq 5$. Or $x - 2 \leq -3 \to x \leq -3 + 2 \to x \leq -1$

Then, solution is: $x \geq 5 \cup x \leq -1$

54) Choice E is correct

Based on triangle similarity theorem: $\frac{a}{a+b} = \frac{c}{3} \to c = \frac{3a}{a+b} = \frac{3\sqrt{3}}{3\sqrt{3}} = 1 \to$ area of shaded region is:
$\left(\frac{c+3}{2}\right)(b) = \frac{4}{2} \times 2\sqrt{3} = 4\sqrt{3}$

55) Choice A is correct

The quadrilateral is a trapezoid. Use the formula of the area of trapezoids. $Area = \frac{1}{2}h(b_1 + b_2)$

You can find the height of the trapezoid by finding the difference of the values of y for the points A and D. (or points B and C). You can also find the distance of A and B by finding the difference of the values of x for the points A and B. Use same method to find the distance of D and C.
$$h = 8 - 2 = 5, \qquad AB = 5 - 2 = 3, \qquad CD = 7 - 1 = 6$$

Area of the trapezoid is: $\frac{1}{2}h(b_1 + b_2) = \frac{1}{2}(5)(3 + 6) = 22.5$

56) Choice C is correct

Choose a random number for n and check the options. Let n be equal to 9 which is divisible by 3, then:

A. $n - 2 = 9 - 2 = 7$ is not divisible by 2
B. $n + 2 = 9 + 2 = 11$ is not divisible by 2
C. $2n + 2 = 2 \times 9 = 188$ is divisible by 2. Try 15, 21, … . For all values of n, $2n + 2$ is divisible by 2.
D. $2n - 1 = (2 \times 9) - 1 = 17$ is not divisible by 2.
E. $3n - 2 = 3(9) - 2 = 27 - 2 = 25$ is not divisible by 2.

Praxis Core Math Practice Test 5

1) Choice C is correct

Plug in the value of x and y: $x = 2$ and $y = -1$

$2(2x - y) + (4 - x)^2 = x^2 - 4x - 2y + 16 = (2)^2 - 4(2) - 2(-1) + 16 = 14$

2) Choice E is correct

Use formula of rectangle prism volume : $V = (length)(width)(height) \Rightarrow 1,500 = (15)(10)(height) \Rightarrow height = 1,500 \div 150 = 10$

3) Choice C is correct

To find the number of possible outfit combinations, multiply number of options for each factor: $5 \times 4 \times 3 = 60$

4) Choice E is correct

$g(x) = 3$, then $f(g(x)) = f(3) = (3)^3 - 2(3)^2 + 8(3) = 27 - 18 + 24 = 33$

5) Choice E is correct

Let x be the width of the rectangle. Use Pythagorean Theorem:

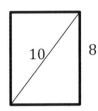

$a^2 + b^2 = c^2$

$x^2 + 8^2 = 10^2 \Rightarrow x^2 + 64 = 100 \Rightarrow x^2 = 100 - 64 = 36 \Rightarrow x = 6$

Perimeter of the rectangle $= 2(length + width) = 2(8 + 6) = 2(14) = 28$

6) Choices D and E are correct

(If you selected 3 choices and 2 of them are correct, then you get one point. If you answered 2 or 3 choices and one of them is correct, you receive one point. If you selected more than 3 choices, you won't get any point for this question.)

Some of prime numbers are: $2, 3, 5, 7, 11, 13$. Find the product of two consecutive prime numbers: $2 \times 3 = 6$ (not in the options), $3 \times 5 = 15$ (bingo!), $5 \times 7 = 35$ (yes!) ,$7 \times 11 = 77$ (not in the options). Choices D and E are correct.

7) Choice C is correct

Solve for the sum of seven numbers: $average = \dfrac{sum\ of\ terms}{number\ of\ terms} \Rightarrow 32 = \dfrac{sum\ of\ 7\ numbers}{7} \Rightarrow$ $sum\ of\ 7\ numbers = 32 \times 7 = 224$, The sum of 7 numbers is 224. If a eighth number 18 is added, then the sum of 8 numbers is :

$224 + 18 = 242$, $average = \dfrac{sum\ of\ terms}{number\ of\ terms} = \dfrac{242}{8} = 30.25$

8) Choice C is correct

Th ratio of boy to girls is $4 : 7$. Therefore, there are 4 boys out of 11 students. To find the answer, first divide the total number of students by 11, then multiply the result by 4.

$44 \div 11 = 4 \Rightarrow 4 \times 4 = 16$, There are 16 boys and $28(44 - 16)$ girls. So, 12 more boys should be enrolled to make the ratio $1 : 1$

9) Choice D is correct

Isolate and solve for x: $\dfrac{2}{3}x + \dfrac{1}{6} = \dfrac{1}{3} \Rightarrow \dfrac{2}{3}x = \dfrac{1}{3} - \dfrac{1}{6} = \dfrac{1}{6} \Rightarrow \dfrac{2}{3}x = \dfrac{1}{6}$

Multiply both sides by the reciprocal of the coefficient of x.

$(\dfrac{3}{2})\dfrac{2}{3}x = \dfrac{1}{6}(\dfrac{3}{2}) \Rightarrow x = \dfrac{3}{12} = \dfrac{1}{4}$

10) Choice B is correct

Use simple interest formula: $I = prt$, ($I = interest, p = principal, r = rate, t = time$)

$I = (16,000)(0.025)(3) = 1,200$

11) Choice E is correct

Jason needs an 75% average to pass for five exams. Therefore, the sum of 5 exams must be at lease $5 \times 75 = 375$, The sum of 4 exams is: $68 + 72 + 85 + 90 = 315$.

The minimum score Jason can earn on his fifth and final test to pass is: $375 - 315 = 60$

12) Choice D is correct

To get a sum of 6 for two dice, we can get 5 different options: $(5, 1), (4, 2), (3, 3), (2, 4), (1, 5)$

To get a sum of 9 for two dice, we can get 4 different options: $(6, 3), (5, 4), (4, 5), (3, 6)$

Therefore, there are 9 options to get the sum of 6 or 9. Since, we have $6 \times 6 = 36$ total options, the probability of getting a sum of 6 and 9 is 9 out of 36 or $\frac{1}{4}$.

13) Choices D and E are correct

(If you selected 3 choices and 2 of them are correct, then you get one point. If you answered 2 or 3 choices and one of them is correct, you receive one point. If you selected more than 3 choices, you won't get any point for this question.)

Simplify the inequality: $2y + 6 < 30 \rightarrow 2y < 30 - 6 \rightarrow 2y < 24 \rightarrow y < 12$. Only choices D (8) and E (-12) are less than 12.

14) Choice D is correct

Use FOIL method: $(3x - y)(2x + 2y) = 6x^2 + 6xy - 2xy - 2y^2 = 6x^2 + 4xy - 2y^2$

15) Choice D is correct

To solve absolute values equations, write two equations. $x - 12$ could be positive 4, or negative -4. Therefore, $x - 12 = 4 \Rightarrow x = 16$, $x - 12 = -4 \Rightarrow x = 8$. Find the product of solutions: $8 \times 16 = 128$

16) Choice B is correct

The equation of a line in slope intercept form is: $y = mx + b$

Solve for y: $4x - 2y = 12 \Rightarrow -2y = 12 - 4x \Rightarrow y = (12 - 4x) \div (-2) \Rightarrow$

$y = 2x - 6$, The slope is 2, The slope of the line perpendicular to this line is:

$m_1 \times m_2 = -1 \Rightarrow 2 \times m_2 = -1 \Rightarrow m_2 = -\frac{1}{2}$

17) Choice C is correct

Three times of 18,000 is 54,000. One sixth of them cancelled their tickets.

One sixth of 54,000 equals 9,000 ($\frac{1}{6} \times 54,000 = 9,000$).

45,000 ($54,000 - 9,000 = 45,000$) fans are attending this week.

18) Choice E is correct

The area of the square is 81 inches. Therefore, the side of the square is square root of the area. $\sqrt{81} = 9$ inches. Four times the side of the square is the perimeter: $4 \times 9 = 36\ inches$

19) Choice E is correct

First factor the function: $(x - 4)(x - 3)$. To find the zeros, $f(x)$ should be zero: $f(x) = (x - 4)(x - 3) = 0$, Therefore, the zeros are, $(x - 4) = 0 \Rightarrow x = 4, (x - 3) = 0 \Rightarrow x = 3$

20) Choice C is correct

$$average\ (mean) = \frac{sum\ of\ terms}{number\ of\ terms} \Rightarrow 88 = \frac{sum\ of\ terms}{50} \Rightarrow sum = 88 \times 50 = 4400$$

The difference of 94 and 69 is 25. Therefore, 25 should be subtracted from the sum.

$$4400 - 25 = 4375, mean = \frac{sum\ of\ terms}{number\ of\ terms} \Rightarrow mean = \frac{4375}{50} = 87.5$$

21) Choice B is correct

Plug in 122 for F and then solve for C.

$$C = \frac{5}{9}(F - 32) \Rightarrow C = \frac{5}{9}(122 - 32) \Rightarrow C = \frac{5}{9}(90) = 50$$

22) Choice A is correct

The width of the rectangle is twice its length. Let x be the length. Then, $width = 2x$

Perimeter of the rectangle is: $2\ (width + length) = 2(2x + x) = 120 \Rightarrow 6x = 120 \Rightarrow x = 20$. Length of the rectangle is 20 meters.

23) Choice A is correct

First, find the number. Let x be the number. Write the equation and solve for x.

150% of a number is 75, then: $1.5 \times x = 75 \Rightarrow x = 75 \div 1.5 = 50$. 90% of 50 is: $0.9 \times 50 = 45$

24) Choice E is correct

Solve for y: $8x - 4y = 8$, Divided both sides by -4: $\frac{8}{-4}x - \frac{4}{-4}y = \frac{8}{-4}$

$-2x + y = -2 \rightarrow y = 2x - 2$, Then: The slope of the line is 2.

25) Choice C is correct

The population is increased by 12% and 25%. 12% increase changes the population to 112% of original population. For the second increase, multiply the result by 125%: $(1.12) \times (1.25) = 1.40 = 140\%$, 40 percent of the population is increased after two years.

26) Choice D is correct

$$average = \frac{sum\ of\ terms}{number\ of\ terms} \Rightarrow (\text{average of 8 numbers})\ 14 = \frac{sum\ of\ numbers}{8} \Rightarrow sum\ of\ 8$$
numbers is: $14 \times 8 = 112$

(average of 6 numbers) $12 = \frac{\text{sum of numbers}}{6} \Rightarrow$ sum of 6 numbers is: $12 \times 6 = 72$

sum of 8 numbers $-$ sum of 6 numbers $=$ sum of 2 numbers

$112 - 72 = 40$ average of 2 numbers $= \frac{40}{2} = 20$

27) Choice E is correct

Five years ago, Amy was three times as old as Mike. Mike is 10 years now. Therefore, 5 years ago Mike was 5 years. Five years ago, Amy was: $A = 3 \times 5 = 15$, Now Amy is 20 years old: $15 + 5 = 20$

28) Choice C is correct

Write a proportion and solve for x: $\frac{4}{3} = \frac{x}{18} \Rightarrow 3x = 18 \times 4 \Rightarrow x = \frac{72}{3} = 24\ ft$

29) Choice A is correct.

Let the number be A. Then: $x = y\% \times A$. Solve for A. $x = \frac{y}{100} \times A$

Multiply both sides by $\frac{100}{y}$: $x \times \frac{100}{y} = \frac{y}{100} \times \frac{100}{y} \times A \rightarrow A = \frac{100x}{y}$

30) The answer is-3.

Use PEMDAS (order of operation): $-15 + 6 \times (-5) - [4 + 22 \times (-4)] \div 2 =$

$$-15 - 30 - [4 - 88] \div 2 = -45 - [-84] \div 2 = -45 + 84 \div 2 = -45 + 42 = -3$$

31) Choice A is correct

One liter $= 1000$ cm$^3 \rightarrow 6$ liters $= 6000$ cm^3

$6000 = 15 \times 5 \times h \rightarrow h = \frac{6000}{75} = 80$ cm

32) Choice B is correct

$\frac{2}{3} \times 90 = 60$

33) Choice C is correct

I. $|a| < 1 \rightarrow -1 < a < 1$

Multiply all sides by b. Since, $b > 0 \rightarrow -b < ba < b$ (it is true!)

II. Since, $-1 < a < 1, and\ a < 0 \rightarrow -a > a^2 > a$ (plug in $-\frac{1}{2}$, and check!) (It's false)

III. $-1 < a < 1, multiply\ all\ sides\ by\ 2, then: -2 < 2a < 2$

Subtract 3 from all sides. Then: $-2 - 3 < 2a - 3 < 2 - 3 \rightarrow -5 < 2a - 3 < -1$ (It is true!)

34) Choice E is correct

Use Pythagorean Theorem: $a^2 + b^2 = c^2$

$80^2 + 150^2 = c^2 \Rightarrow 6400 + 22500 = c^2 \Rightarrow 28900 = c^2 \Rightarrow c = 170$

35) Choice C is correct

Let x be the number. Write the equation and solve for x.

$30\% \ of \ x = 12 \Rightarrow 0.30x = 12 \Rightarrow x = 12 \div 0.30 = 40$

36) Choice C is correct

The distance between Jason and Joe is 15 miles. Jason running at 4.5 miles per hour and Joe is running at the speed of 7 miles per hour. Therefore, every hour the distance is 2.5 miles less. $15 \div 2.5 = 6$

37) Choice D is correct

The failing rate is 11 out of $55 = \frac{11}{55}$, Change the fraction to percent: $\frac{11}{55} \times 100\% = 20\%$

20 percent of students failed. Therefore, 80 percent of students passed the exam.

38) Choice D is correct

A. $f(x) = x^2 - 5$ if $x = 1 \rightarrow f(1) = (1)^2 - 5 = 1 - 5 = -4 \neq 5$

B. $f(x) = x^2 - 1$ if $x = 1 \rightarrow f(1) = (1)^2 - 1 = 1 - 1 = 0 \neq 5$

C. $f(x) = \sqrt{x+2}$ if $x = 1 \rightarrow f(1) = \sqrt{1+2} = \sqrt{3} \neq 5$

D. $f(x) = \sqrt{x} + 4$ if $x = 1 \rightarrow f(1) = \sqrt{1} + 4 = 5$

E. $f(x) = \sqrt{x+1} + 4$ if $x = 1 \rightarrow f(1) = \sqrt{1+1} + 4 \neq 5$

39) Choice B is correct

Plug in $z/3$ for z and simplify.

$$x_1 = \frac{8y + \frac{r}{r+1}}{\frac{\frac{z}{3}}{6}} = \frac{8y + \frac{r}{r+1}}{\frac{3 \times 6}{z}} = \frac{8y + \frac{r}{r+1}}{3 \times \frac{6}{z}} = \frac{1}{3} \times \frac{8y + \frac{r}{r+1}}{\frac{6}{z}} = \frac{x}{3}$$

40) The answer is 600.

Let b be the amount of time Alec can do the job and let a be the amount of time Michelle can do the job. Then: $\frac{1}{a} + \frac{1}{b} = \frac{1}{200} \rightarrow \frac{1}{300} + \frac{1}{b} = \frac{1}{200} \rightarrow \frac{1}{b} = \frac{1}{200} - \frac{1}{300} = \frac{1}{600}$

Then: $b = 600$ minutes

41) Choice D is correct

Solve for x: $x^3 + 18 = 130 \rightarrow x^3 = 112$

Let's review the choices.

A. 1 and 2. $1^3 = 1$ and $2^3 = 8$, 112 is not between these two numbers.

B. 2 and 3. $2^3 = 8$ and $3^3 = 27$, 112 is not between these two numbers.

C. 3 and 4. $3^3 = 27$ and $4^3 = 64$, 112 is not between these two numbers.

D. 4 and 5. $4^3 = 64$ and $5^3 = 125$, 112 is between these two numbers.

E. 5 and 6. $5^3 = 125$ and $6^3 = 126$, 112 is not between these two numbers.

42) Choice B is correct.

Solve for x: $\frac{3x}{25} = \frac{x-1}{5}$, Multiply the second fraction by 5: $\frac{3x}{25} = \frac{5(x-1)}{5 \times 5}$

Tow denominators are equal. Therefore, the numerators must be equal.

$3x = 5x - 5 \rightarrow -2x = -5 \rightarrow \frac{5}{2} = x$

43) Choice D is correct

$(x-2)^3 = 27 \rightarrow x - 2 = 3 \rightarrow x = 5. \rightarrow (x-6)(x-4) = (5-6)(5-4) = (-1)(1) = -1$

44) The answer is 5.

Solving Systems of Equations by Elimination

$\begin{array}{l} 3x - 4y = -20 \\ -x + 2y = 10 \end{array}$ Multiply the second equation by 3, then add it to the first equation.

$\begin{array}{l} 3x - 4y = -20 \\ 3(-x + 2y = 10) \end{array} \Rightarrow \begin{array}{l} 3x - 4y = -20 \\ -3x + 6y = 30) \end{array} \Rightarrow 2y = 10 \Rightarrow y = 5$

45) Choice C is correct

First find the value of b, and then find $f(3)$. Since $f(2) = 35$, substuting 2 for x and 35 for $f(x)$ gives $35 = b(2)^2 + 15 = 4b + 15$. Solving this equation gives $b = 5$. Thus

$f(x) = 5x^2 + 15, \quad f(3) = 5(3)^2 + 15 \rightarrow f(3) = 45 + 15, \quad f(3) = 60$

46) Choice A is correct

Identify the input value. Since the function is in the form $f(x)$ and the question asks to calculate $f(3)$, the input value is four. $f(3) \rightarrow x = 3$ Using the function, input the desired x value.

Now substitute 4 in for every x in the function. $f(x) = 3x^2 - 5, \quad f(3) = 3(3)^2 - 5,$

$f(3) = 27 - 5, \quad f(3) = 22$

47) Choice D is correct

Frist factor the function: $f(x) = x^3 + 8x^2 + 12x = x(x+2)(x+6)$, To find the zeros, $f(x)$ should be zero. $f(x) = x(x+2)(x+6) = 0$, Therefore, the zeros are: $x = 0, \quad (x+2) = 0 \Rightarrow x = -2, (x+6) = 0 \Rightarrow x = -6$

48) Choice C is correct

Since, E is the midpoint of AB, then the area of all triangles DAE, DEF, CFE and CBE are equal. Let x be the area of one of the triangle, then: $4x = 100 \rightarrow x = 25$

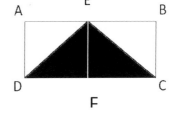

The area of $DEC = 2x = 2(25) = 50$

49) Choice D is correct

The x-intercepts of the parabola represented by $y = x^2 - 9x + 14$ in the xy-plane are the values of x for which y is equal to 0. The factored form of the equation, $y = (x - 2)(x - 7)$, shows that y equals 0 if and only if $x = 2$ or $x = 7$. Thus, the factored form $y = (x - 2)(x - 7)$, displays the x-intercepts of the parabola as the constants 2 and 7.

50) Choice C is correct

If $x - a$ is a factor of $g(x)$, then $g(a)$ must equal 0. Based on the table $g(-2) = 0$. Therefore, $x - (-2)$ or $x + 2$ must be a factor of $g(x)$.

51) Choice C is correct

To solve this problem first solve the equation for c. $\frac{c}{b} = 2$

Multiply by b on both sides. Then: $b \times \frac{c}{b} = 2 \times b \rightarrow c = 2b$. Now to calculate $\frac{8b}{c}$, substitute the value for c into the denominator and simplify. $\frac{8b}{c} = \frac{8b}{2b} = \frac{8}{2} = 4$

52) Choice B is correct

$$\frac{1\frac{4}{3}+\frac{1}{4}}{2\frac{1}{2}-\frac{17}{8}} = \frac{\frac{7}{3}+\frac{1}{4}}{\frac{5}{2}-\frac{17}{8}} = \frac{\frac{28+3}{12}}{\frac{20-17}{8}} = \frac{\frac{31}{12}}{\frac{3}{8}} = \frac{31\times8}{12\times3} = \frac{31\times2}{3\times3} = \frac{62}{9} \cong 6.88$$

53) Choice A is correct

First write the equation in slope intercept form. Add $2x$ to both sides to get $y = 2x + 36$. The slope of this line is 2, so any line that also has a slope of 2 would be parallel to it. Only choice A has a slope of 2.

54) Choice C is correct

40% of 60 equals to: $0.40 \times 60 = 24$. 12% of 600 equals to: $0.12 \times 600 = 72$

40% of 60 is added to 12% of 600: $24 + 72 = 96$

55) Choice A is correct

$|x - 2| \geq 4$. Then: $x - 2 \geq 4$ or $x - 2 \leq 4$. Solve both inequalities: $x - 2 \geq 4 \rightarrow x \geq 6$ and $x - 2 \leq 4 \rightarrow x \leq 6$. The solution of the inequality $|x - 2| \geq 4$ is $x \geq 6 \cup x \leq -2$

56) Choice B is correct.

Simplify the expression. $\sqrt{\frac{x^2}{2} + \frac{x^2}{16}} = \sqrt{\frac{8x^2}{16} + \frac{x^2}{16}} = \sqrt{\frac{9x^2}{16}} = \sqrt{\frac{9}{16}x^2} = \sqrt{\frac{9}{16}} \times \sqrt{x^2} = \frac{3}{4} \times x = \frac{3x}{4}$

"Effortless Math Education" Publications

Effortless Math authors' team strives to prepare and publish the best quality Praxis Core Math learning resources to make learning Math easier for all. We hope that our publications help you learn Math in an effective way and prepare for the Praxis Core test.

We all in Effortless Math wish you good luck and successful studies!

Effortless Math Authors

www.EffortlessMath.com

... So Much More Online!

✓ FREE Math lessons

✓ More Math learning books!

✓ Mathematics Worksheets

✓ Online Math Tutors

Need a PDF version of this book?

Visit www.EffortlessMath.com

Receive the PDF version of this book or get another FREE book!

Thank you for using our Book!

Do you LOVE this book?

Then, you can get the PDF version of this book or another book absolutely FREE!

Please email us at:

info@EffortlessMath.com

for details.

Made in the USA
Columbia, SC
03 March 2021